Table of Contents

Table of Contents

Name: _____

Place Value

Place value is the position of a digit in a number. A digit's place in a number shows its value. Numbers left of the decimal point represent **whole numbers**. Numbers right of the decimal point represent a part, or fraction, of a whole number. These parts are broken down into tenths, hundredths, thousandths, and so on.

Example:

3,443,221.621

millions	hundred thousands	ten thousands	thousands	hundreds	tens	ones	tenths	hundredths	thousandths
3	4	4	3	2	2	1	6	2	1

←————————— **Whole Numbers** —————————→ ←——— **Fractions** ———→

Directions: Write the following number words as numbers.

1. Three million, forty-four thousand, six hundred twenty-one _____

2. One million, seventy-seven _____

3. Nine million, six hundred thousand, one hundred two _____

4. Twenty-nine million, one hundred three thousand and nine tenths

_____

5. One million, one hundred thousand, one hundred seventy-one and

thirteen hundredths _____

Directions: In each box, write the corresponding number for each place value.

1. 4,822,000.00   ☐ hundreds

2. 55,907,003.00   ☐ thousands

3. 190,641,225.07   ☐ hundred thousands

4. 247,308,211.59   ☐ tenths

5. 7,594,097.33   ☐ millions

6. 201,480,110.01   ☐ hundred thousands

7. 42,367,109,074.25 ☐ hundredths

Place Value

The chart below shows the place value of each number.

trillions			billions			millions			thousands			ones		
h	t	o	h	t	o	h	t	o	h	t	o	h	t	o
		2	1	4	0	9	0	0	6	8	0	3	5	0

Word form: two trillion, one hundred forty billion, nine hundred million, six hundred eighty thousand, three hundred fifty

Directions: Draw a line to the correct value of each underlined digit. The first one is done for you.

6<u>4</u>3,000	2 hundred million
<u>1</u>3,294,125	9 billion
<u>6</u>78,446	40 thousand
389,<u>2</u>76	2 thousand
1<u>9</u>,000,089,965	2 billion
78,<u>7</u>64	1 hundred thousand
61<u>2</u>,689	9 thousand
<u>2</u>98,154,370	70 thousand
8<u>9</u>,256	10 million
1,<u>3</u>70	30 million
853,6<u>7</u>2,175	7 hundred
<u>2</u>,842,751,360	3 hundred
<u>1</u>63,456	2 hundred
4<u>3</u>8,276,587	6 hundred thousand

Name: _____

Expanded Notation

Expanded notation is writing out the value of each digit in a number.

Example:
8,920,077 = 8,000,000 + 900,000 + 20,000 + 70 + 7
Word form: Eight million, nine hundred twenty thousand, seventy-seven

Directions: Write the following numbers using expanded notation.

1. 20,769,033 _____

_____

2. 1,183,541,029 _____

_____

3. 776,003,091 _____

_____

4. 5,920,100,808 _____

_____

5. 14,141,543,760 _____

_____

Directions: Write the following numbers.

1. 700,000 + 900 + 60 + 7 _____

2. 35,000,000 + 600,000 + 400 + 40 + 2 _____

3. 12,000,000 + 700,000 + 60,000 + 4,000 + 10 + 4 _____

4. 80,000,000,000 + 8,000,000,000 + 400,000,000 + 80,000,000 + 10,000 + 400 + 30

_____

5. 4,000,000,000 + 16,000,000 + 30 + 2 _____

© 2001 McGraw-Hill.

Addition and Place Value

Directions: Add the problems below in which the digits with the same place value are lined up correctly. Then cross out the problems in which the digits are not lined up correctly.

Find each answer in the diagram and color that section.

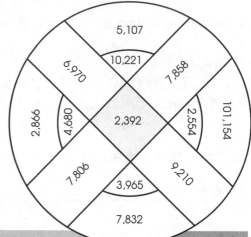

yellow	blue	green	red
638 1,289 + 465 —— 2,392	~~98 324 + 9,756~~	4,326 82 + 699	589 95 + 8,526
579 125 + 244	296 2,183 + 75	93,287 36 + 7,831	51 315 + 7,492
83 1,298 + 62	938 3,297 + 445	1,849 964 + 53	198 72 + 68
987 934 + 3,163	46 390 + 9,785	856 642 + 7,462	591 6,352 + 27
57 7,520 + 463	773 3,118 + 74	64 7,430 + 338	919 52 + 6,835

Diagram sections: 5,107; 10,221; 6,970; 7,858; 2,866; 4,680; 2,392; 2,554; 101,154; 7,806; 3,965; 9,210; 7,832

Name: _____

Addition

Directions: Add the following numbers.

88	27	91	76	54	29
+ 16	+ 24	+ 59	+ 35	+ 37	+ 48

13	28	41	33	7	39
27	44	98	17	25	86
+ 82	+ 56	+ 72	+ 75	+ 60	+ 94

5,943	3,031	7,280	1,258	6,711
+ 2,075	+ 5,187	+ 1,945	+ 5,290	+ 5,088

9,227	8,314	5,693	2,500	3,741
1,243	702	407	4,693	9,205
+ 5,012	+ 7,218	+ 3,920	+ 7,055	+ 368

Name: _____

Addition

Directions: Add the following numbers in your head without writing them out.

1. 17 + 33 = _____   2. 35 + 15 = _____   3. 75 + 25 = _____

4. 41 + 25 = _____   5. 27 + 23 = _____   6. 30 + 20 = _____

7. 12 + 18 = _____   8. 43 + 22 = _____   9. 16 + 34 = _____

10. 9 + 11 + 30 = _____   11. 29 + 21 + 40 = _____

12. 14 + 16 + 20 = _____   13. 37 + 13 + 25 = _____

14. 12 + 22 + 36 = _____   15. 19 + 21 + 57 = _____

16. 21 + 24 + 25 = _____   17. 63 + 14 + 11 = _____

18. 33 + 15 + 42 = _____   19. 25 + 15 + 60 = _____

20. 30 + 20 + 10 = _____

$$14 + 12 + 7 + 20 + 9 + 18 = ?$$

Name: _____

Addition Word Problems

Directions: Solve the following addition word problems.

1. 100 students participated in a sports card show in the school gym. Brad brought his entire collection of 2,000 cards to show his friends. He had 700 football cards and 400 basketball cards. If the rest of his cards were baseball cards, how many baseball cards did he bring with him?

   _____

2. Refreshments were set up in one area of the gym. Hot dogs were a dollar, soda was 50 cents, chips were 35 cents and cookies were a quarter. If you purchased two of each item, how much money would you need?

   _____

3. It took each student 30 minutes to set up for the card show and twice as long to put everything away. The show was open for 3 hours. How much time did each student spend on this event?

   _____

4. 450 people attended the card show. 55 were mothers of students, 67 were fathers, 23 were grandparents, 8 were aunts and uncles and the rest were kids. How many kids attended?

   _____

5. Of the 100 students who set up displays, most of them sold or traded some of their cards. Bruce sold 75 cards, traded 15 cards and collected $225. Kevin only sold 15 cards, traded 81 cards and collected $100. Missi traded 200 cards, sold 10 and earned $35. Of those listed, how many cards were sold, how many were traded and how much money was earned?

   sold _____   traded _____   earned $ _____

© 2001 McGraw-Hill.

Name: _____

Subtraction

Directions: Subtract the following numbers. When subtracting, begin on the right, especially if you need to regroup and borrow.

549 − 162	823 − 417	370 − 244	648 − 79
700 − 343	475 − 299	603 − 425	354 − 265
1,841 − 952	2,597 − 608	6,832 − 1,774	9,005 − 3,458
23,342 − 9,093	53,790 − 40,813	29,644 − 19,780	35,726 − 16,959
109,432 − 79,145	350,907 − 14,185	217,523 − 44,197	537,411 − 406,514

Name: _____

Subtraction

Directions: Subtract the following numbers in your head without writing them out.

1. 22 – 11 = _____   2. 55 – 25 = _____   3. 83 – 22 = _____

4. 36 – 14 = _____   5. 68 – 17 = _____   6. 70 – 34 = _____

7. 77 – 32 = _____   8. 94 – 50 = _____   9. 85 – 16 = _____

10. 42 – 21 = _____   11. 53 – 23 = _____

12. 95 – 30 = _____   13. 135 – 65 = _____

14. 316 – 10 = _____   15. 248 – 22 = _____

16. 747 – 525 = _____   17. 495 – 255 = _____

18. 815 – 312 = _____   19. 410 – 220 = _____

20. 347 – 120 = _____   21. 726 – 529 = _____

22. 920 – 721 = _____   23. 1,220 – 410 = _____

24. 3,475 – 1,200 = _____   25. 2,116 – 1,072 = _____

26. 4,750 – 4,725 = _____   27. 1,170 – 1,135 = _____

28. 5,621 – 875 = _____   29. 8,765 – 3,748 = _____

30. 10,011 – 728 = _____   31. 17,780 – 6,213 = _____

32. 32,360 – 32,160 = _____   33. 1,000,000 – 500,000 = _____

Subtraction Word Problems

Directions: Solve the following subtraction word problems.

1. Last year, 28,945 people lived in Mike's town. This year there are 31,889. How many people have moved in? _____

2. Brad earned $227 mowing lawns. He spent $168 on tapes by his favorite rock group. How much money does he have left? _____

3. The school year has 180 days. Carrie has gone to 32 school days so far. How many more days does she have left? _____

4. Craig wants a skateboard that costs $128. He has saved $47. How much more does he need? _____

5. To get to school, Jennifer walks 1,275 steps and Carolyn walks 2,618 steps. How many more steps does Carolyn walk than Jennifer? _____

6. Amy has placed 91 of the 389 pieces in a new puzzle she purchased. How many more does she have left to finish? _____

7. From New York, it's 2,823 miles to Los Angeles and 1,327 miles to Miami. How much farther away is Los Angeles? _____

8. Sheila read that a piece of carrot cake has 236 calories, but a piece of apple pie has 427 calories. How many calories will she save by eating the cake instead of the pie? _____

9. Tim's summer camp costs $223, while Sam's costs $149. How much more does Tim's camp cost?

   _____

10. Last year, the nation's budget was $45,000,000,000, but the nation spent $52,569,342,000. How much more than its budget did the nation spend?

    _____

Name: _____

Multiplication

Directions: Multiply the following numbers. Be sure to keep the numbers aligned, and place a 0 in the ones place.

Example:	Correct	Incorrect
	55	55
	x 15	x 15
	275	275
	550	55
	825	330

1. 12
   x 6

2. 44
   x 9

3. 27
   x 7

4. 92
   x 6

5. 85
   x 9

6. 78
   x 24

7. 32
   x 17

8. 19
   x 46

9. 63
   x 12

10. 38
    x 77

11. 125
    x 6

12. 641
    x 25

13. 713
    x 47

14. 586
    x 45

15. 294
    x 79

16. 20 x 4 x 7 = _____

17. 9 x 5 x 11 = _____

18. 16 x 2 x 2 = _____

19. 7 x 6 x 3 = _____

20. 33 x 11 x 3 = _____

21. 2 x 8 x 10 = _____

MATH 6

Multiplication Word Problems

Directions: Solve the following multiplication word problems. Remember to multiply the ones first, then the tens, then the hundreds.

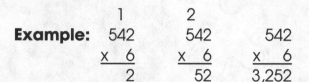

	1	2	
Example:	542	542	542
	x 6	x 6	x 6
	2	52	3,252

1. Angela bought 6 tapes for $12 each. How much did she spend? _____

2. Steve finished 9 pages of math with 24 problems on each page. How many problems did he do?
   _____

3. Dana sold 27 boxes of candy for $3 each, but she thinks she may have lost some of the money. How much money should she have? _____

4. Nathan rides his bike 4 miles to school every day. How far will he ride in 31 days? _____

5. Julie swam the length of the pool 7 times. It took her 31 seconds each time. How many seconds did she swim altogether? _____

6. In Derek's scout group, 4 boys have earned 14 badges each. How many badges have they earned altogether? _____

7. For a school party, 7 families sent in a dozen cookies each. How many cookies in all were sent? _____

8. Matt mowed 8 lawns for $11 each. Tito mowed 12 lawns for $9 each. Who made more money, and how much more did he make? _____

9. The teacher needed 14 volunteers to work 3 hours each. How many hours of help did he need? _____

10. The city's stadium, which has 14,900 seats, was sold out for 6 baseball games last summer. How many people came to those games? _____

Name: _____

Multiplying With Zeros

Directions: Multiply the following numbers. If a number ends with zero, you can eliminate it while calculating the rest of the answer. Then count how many zeros you took off and add them to your answer.

Example:	55̶0̶	Take off 2 zeros	50̶0̶	Take off 2 zeros
	x 5̶0̶		x 5	
	27,5̲0̲0̲	Add on 2 zeros	2,5̲0̲0̲	Add on 2 zeros

1. 300
   x 6

2. 400
   x 7

3. 620
   x 5

4. 290
   x 7

5. 142
   x 20

6. 505
   x 50

7. 340
   x 70

8. 600
   x 60

9. 550
   x 380

10. 290
    x 150

11. 2,040
    x 360

12. 8,800
    x 200

13. Bruce traveled 600 miles each day of a 10-day trip. How far did he go during the entire trip? _____

14. 30 children each sold 20 items for the school fund-raiser. Each child earned $100 for the school. How much money did the school collect? _____

15. 10 x 40 x 2 = _____

16. 30 x 30 x 10 = _____

17. 100 x 60 x 10 = _____

18. 500 x 11 x 2 = _____

19. 9 x 10 x 10 = _____

20. 7,000 x 20 x 10 = _____

Division

In a division problem, the **dividend** is the number to be divided, the **divisor** is the number used to divide and the **quotient** is the answer. To check your work, multiply your answer times the divisor and you should get the dividend.

Example: 130 ← **quotient**   **Check:**   130 ← **quotient**
divisor → 4$\overline{)520}$ ← **dividend**   x   4 ← **divisor**
                 4   520 ← **dividend**
               $\overline{}$12
                 12
               $\overline{}$00

Directions: Solve the following division problems.

1. 3$\overline{)546}$ 2. 5$\overline{)720}$ 3. 2$\overline{)458}$ 4. 4$\overline{)796}$ 5. 7$\overline{)896}$

6. 4$\overline{)128}$ 7. 4$\overline{)376}$ 8. 5$\overline{)225}$ 9. 3$\overline{)684}$ 10. 6$\overline{)924}$

11. 25$\overline{)475}$ 12. 16$\overline{)768}$ 13. 14$\overline{)840}$ 14. 22$\overline{)418}$ 15. 21$\overline{)693}$

Directions: Solve these division problems in your head. Challenge yourself for speed and accuracy.

1. $22 \div 2 =$ _____   2. $15 \div 3 =$ _____   3. $72 \div 9 =$ _____

4. $36 \div 4 =$ _____   5. $27 \div 9 =$ _____   6. $56 \div 8 =$ _____

7. $81 \div 9 =$ _____   8. $42 \div 6 =$ _____   9. $63 \div 9 =$ _____

10. $60 \div 5 =$ _____   11. $70 \div 10 =$ _____   12. $98 \div 7 =$ _____

13. $55 \div 5 =$ _____   14. $64 \div 8 =$ _____   15. $84 \div 3 =$ _____

Name:_____

Division Word Problems

In the example below, 368 is being divided by 4. 4 won't divide into 3, so move over one position and divide 4 into 36. 4 goes into 36 nine times. Then multiply 4 x 9 to get 36. Subtract 36 from 36. The answer is 0, less than the divisor, so 9 is the right number. Now bring down the 8, divide 4 into it and repeat the process.

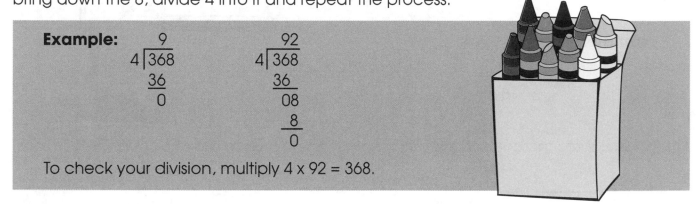

Example:

$$4\overline{)368} = 9, \quad 36, \quad 0$$

$$4\overline{)368} = 92, \quad 36, \quad 08, \quad 8, \quad 0$$

To check your division, multiply 4 x 92 = 368.

Directions: Solve the following division problems. (For some problems, you will also need to add or subtract.)

1. Kristy helped the kindergarten teacher put a total of 192 crayons into 8 boxes. How many crayons did they put into each box?

_____

2. The scout troop has to finish a 12-mile hike in 3 hours. How many miles an hour will they have to walk?

_____

3. At her slumber party, Shelly had 4 friends and 25 pieces of candy. If she kept 5 pieces and divided the rest among her friends, how many pieces did each friend get?

_____

4. Kenny's book has 147 pages. He wants to read the same number of pages each day and finish reading the book in 7 days. How many pages should he read each day?

_____

5. Brian and 2 friends are going to share 27 marbles. How many will each person get?

_____

6. To help the school, 5 parents agreed to sell 485 tickets for a raffle. How many tickets will each person have to sell to do his/her part?

_____

7. Tim is going to weed his neighbor's garden for $3 an hour. How many hours does he have to work to make $72?

_____

Name:_____

Equations

In an **equation**, the value on the left of the equal sign must equal the value on the right. Remember the order of operations: solve from left to right, multiply or divide numbers before adding or subtracting and do the operation inside parentheses first.

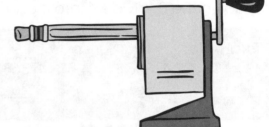

Example:
$$6 + 4 - 2 = 4 \times 2$$
$$10 - 2 \ = \ 8$$
$$8 \ = \ 8$$

Directions: Write the correct operation signs in the blanks to make accurate equations.

1. (25 _____ 25) _____ 2 = 100 _____ 75

2. (76 _____ 24) _____ 3 = 150 _____ 2

3. 140 _____ 2 _____ 10 = 500 _____ 50 _____ 150

4. 2,100 _____ 2,000 _____ 60 = 80 _____ 2

5. 80 _____ 8 _____ 4 = 160 _____ 160 _____ 160

6. 55 _____ 100 _____ 11 = 1,000 _____ 2 _____ 4

7. 137 _____ 81 _____ 52 = 3 _____ 90

8. 3,000 _____ 10 _____ 10 = (600 _____ 300) _____ 30

9. (720 _____ 20) _____ 4 = 37 _____ 5

10. 457 _____ 43 _____ 500 = (21 _____ 40) x 0

Name: _____

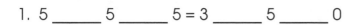

Equations

Directions: Write the correct operation signs in the blanks to make accurate equations.

1. 5 _____ 5 _____ 5 = 3 _____ 5 _____ 0

2. (50 _____ 0) _____ 2 = 25 _____ 2 _____ 2

3. 2 _____ 2 _____ 2 _____ 2 = 2 _____ 2 _____ 4

4. (4 _____ 5) _____ 5 _____ 5 = 2 _____ 3 _____ 5

5. (25 _____ 5) _____ 2 _____ 3 = 3 _____ 6 _____ 2 _____ 5

6. (125 _____ 7) _____ 2 _____ 3 = 100 _____ 2 _____ 4 _____ 70 _____ 10

7. (100 _____ 10) _____ 5 _____ 10 = 10 _____ 5 _____ 100 _____ 10

8. 35 _____ 35 _____ 5 _____ 2 = 5 _____ 3 _____ 2 _____ 5

9. (60 _____ 2) _____ 3 = 3 _____ 3 _____ 3 _____ 0 _____ 15 _____ (5 _____ 15)

10. (120 _____ 4) _____ 7 _____ 3 = (7 _____ 7) _____ (2 _____ 5)

11. 91 _____ 3 _____ 6 _____ 3 = 2 _____ 5 _____ 1 _____ 3 _____ (2 _____ 5)

12. (16 _____ 4) _____ 8 = 5 _____ 5 _____ (3 _____ 3) _____ 6

13. 10 _____ 5 _____ 15 _____ 4 = 3 _____ 3 _____ 3 _____ 8

14. 16 _____ 3 _____ 12 _____ (2 _____ 20) = (2 _____ 2) _____ 6 _____ 10 _____ (2 _____ 7)

15. 21 _____ (3 _____ 3) _____ 3 _____ 1 = 3 _____ 1 _____ 2 _____ 20

Mixed Practice Word Problems

Directions: Read each word problem carefully. Eliminate insignificant information. Determine what you need to know to find the correct answer.

1. 5 cars lined up for the first race of the spring rally. The track was one-half mile long. Each car had to complete 22 laps around the track. How many miles did they travel altogether? _____

2. It took the last car 42 minutes to finish the race. The winner did it in half that time. How long did it take the winner to complete 22 laps around the track? _____

3. During the presentation of awards, they announced that a new record had been set that day. The old record was 185 miles per hour and the new record was 217 miles per hour. How much faster was the new record? _____

4. 1,200 people attended the car rally. All proceeds from the day's events were donated to a local charity. They earned the following amounts of money before expenses:

	Expenses
Admission tickets — $3,600	$400
Concession stand — $2,150	$725
Donations — $325	

   How much were they able to give to charity? _____

5. The local boy scouts and girl scouts offered to clean up the trash after the rally. 40 children arrived to help. 17 of them could only help for 1 hour. Another 12 stayed 2 hours. Combined, it took all the children a total of 74 hours to complete the task. How many hours did each of the other scouts have to help? _____

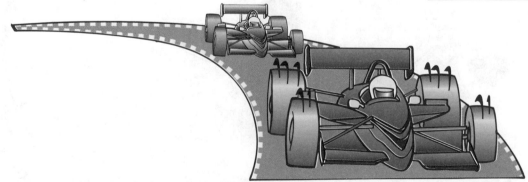

Name: _____

Find the Mean

Mean (the average group of numbers) is a term frequently used for **average** (a value that lies within a range of values). To find the mean, add the numbers, then divide by the number of items.

Directions: Match each mean with the correct number by writing the corresponding letter.

Example: 10 + 20 + 30 = 60   60 ÷ 3 = 20   Mean = 20

Mean

1. 25, 75, 215   _____   A. 775

2. 170, 220, 150   _____   B. 555

3. 390, 465, 810   _____   C. 39

4. 12, 16, 22, 18, 17   _____   D. 1,560

5. 500, 800, 1,200, 600   _____   E. 105

6. 78, 340, 290, 188   _____   F. 2,463

7. 5, 19, 76, 43, 52   _____   G. 510

8. 4,020, 1,368, 2,001   _____   H. 224

9. 640, 935, 1,306, 3,359   _____   I. 180

10. 852, 316, 701, 468, 213   _____   J. 17

Find the mean age of all your family members. Include grandparents, aunts, uncles and cousins.

Name: _____

Averaging

To find an average, add the numbers, then divide by the number of items.

Example: Test scores of 89, 74, and 92:

$$
\begin{array}{r}
89 \\
74 \\
+\,92 \\
\hline
255
\end{array}
\qquad
\begin{array}{r}
85 \\
3\,\overline{)255} \\
\underline{24} \\
15 \\
\underline{15} \\
0
\end{array}
$$

Your average score is **85**.

Directions: Solve each word problem below. (Do your adding and dividing on another sheet of paper.)

1. One bear at the zoo weighs 524 pounds, one weighs 756 pounds and one weighs 982 pounds. What is the average of their total weight? _____

2. Three new cars cost $10,100, $7,800 and $12,400. What is the average cost? _____

3. Paul's school has 684 students, Nicole's has 841 and Kurt's has 497. What is the average number of students at these three schools? _____

4. One street in our neighborhood has 43 houses, one has 26, one has 18 and one has 37. What is the average number of houses per street? _____

5. Lynn has 365 stickers in her collection, Bridget has 343, Karen has 219 and Liz has 141. What is the average number of stickers? _____

6. Four libraries each have this many books: 10,890; 14,594; 9,786; 12,754. What is the average number of books for the libraries? _____

7. Doug found 5 different candy bars with these prices: 45, 65, 90, 85 and 75 cents. What was the average price? _____

8. Four neighboring towns each have this many residents: 6,033; 4,589; 5,867; 1,239. What is the average population of these towns? _____

9. The weekly grocery bill for Jamie's family totaled these amounts for the past 6 weeks: $88, $119, $97, $104, $86 and $112. What does her family spend on groceries, on average? _____

Rounding and Estimating

Rounding is expressing a number to the nearest whole number, ten, thousand or other value.
Estimating is using an approximate number instead of an exact one. When rounding a number, we say a country has 98,000,000 citizens instead of 98,347,425. We can round off numbers to the nearest whole number, the nearest hundred or the nearest million—whatever is appropriate.

Here are the steps: 1) Decide where you want to round off the number. 2) If the digit to the right is less than 5, leave the digit at the rounding place unchanged. 3) If the digit to the right is 5 or more, increase the digit at the rounding place by 1.

> **Examples:** 587 rounded to the nearest hundred is 600.
> 535 rounded to the nearest hundred is 500.
> 21,897 rounded to the nearest thousand is 22,000.
> 21,356 rounded to the nearest thousand is 21,000.
>
> When we estimate numbers, we use rounded, approximate numbers instead of exact ones.
>
> **Example:** A hamburger that costs $1.49 and a drink that costs $0.79 total about $2.30 ($1.50 plus $0.80).

Directions: Use rounding and estimating to find the answers to these questions. You may have to add, subtract, multiply or divide.

1. Debbi is having a party and wants to fill 11 cups from a 67-ounce bottle of pop. About how many ounces should she pour into each cup? _____

2. Tracy studied 28 minutes every day for 4 days. About how long did she study in all? _____

3. About how much does this lunch cost? $1.19 $ 0.39 $ 0.49 _____

4. The numbers below show how long Frank spent studying last week. Estimate how many minutes he studied for the whole week.
Monday: 23 minutes Tuesday: 37 minutes Wednesday: 38 minutes
Thursday: 12 minutes _____

5. One elephant at the zoo weighs 1,417 pounds and another one weighs 1,789 pounds. About how much heavier is the second elephant? _____

6. If Tim studied a total of 122 minutes over 4 days, about how long did he study each day? _____

7. It's 549 miles to Dover and 345 miles to Albany. About how much closer is Albany? _____

MASTER SKILLS
MATH 6

Rounding

Directions: Round off each number, then estimate the answer. You can use a calculator to find the exact answer.

Round to the nearest ten.

	Estimate	Actual Answer
1. $86 \div 9 =$	_____	_____
2. $237 + 488 =$	_____	_____
3. $49 \times 11 =$	_____	_____
4. $309 + 412 =$	_____	_____
5. $625 - 218 =$	_____	_____

Round to the nearest hundred.

6. $790 - 70 =$	_____	_____
7. $690 \div 70 =$	_____	_____
8. $2,177 - 955 =$	_____	_____
9. $4,792 + 3,305 =$	_____	_____
10. $5,210 \times 90 =$	_____	_____

Round to the nearest thousand.

11. $4,078 + 2,093 =$	_____	_____
12. $5,525 - 3,065 =$	_____	_____
13. $6,047 \div 2,991 =$	_____	_____
14. $1,913 \times 4,216 =$	_____	_____
15. $7,227 + 8,449 =$	_____	_____

Name: _____

Review

Directions: Solve the following problems. Round off answers to the nearest hundredth where necessary.

1. Write these numbers in words:

   a. 2,240 _____

   b. 4,873,189 _____

   _____

2. Sara sold 23 glasses of lemonade for 15 cents a glass.
   Beth sold 32 glasses of lemonade for 12 cents a glass.
   Who made more money and how much more did she make?   _____

3. Kent had 4 Superman comic books and 6 times as many Batman
   comic books. How many did he have altogether?   _____

4. Cheryl bought 2 packages of beads with 425 in each package.
   She divided them equally among herself and 4 other people. How
   many beads did each person receive?   _____

5. Four of Eric's guppies had 27 babies each. The next morning he
   could find only 58 baby guppies. How many babies were missing?   _____

6. Mindy made 2 batches of cookies. Each batch had 48 cookies.
   Then she gave all 27 kids in her class 3 cookies each. (She also ate
   3 herself.) How many cookies were left over for her family?   _____

7. Ronnie's family bought a new car that cost $9,000. They made
   a down payment of $1,500. If they pay $250 a month, how many
   months will it take to pay for the car?   _____

8. Estimate how many hours are in a week.   _____

9. Round off these numbers:

   a. To the nearest hundred: 4,328 _____ 7,679 _____

   b. To the nearest thousand: 4,328 _____ 7,679 _____

   c. To the nearest million: 245,763,132 _____

25

Name: _____

Review

Directions: Solve the following problems.

1.   43
     28
   + 92

2.   1,720
     8,341
   + 2,199

3.   485
   − 317

4.   7,241
   − 4,355

5. 23 + 24 + 20 = _____

6. 49 + 11 + 40 = _____

7. 2,400 − 1,250 = _____

8. 3,650 − 2,000 = _____

9.   89
   x 7

10.   342
    x 36

11. 3⟌627 _____

12. 12⟌816 _____

13. 16 x 3 = _____

14. 42 ÷ 7 = _____

15. 24 x 2 = _____

16. 96 ÷ 3 = _____

17. 80 x 11 = _____

18. 84 ÷ 6 = _____

19.   213
    x 50

20. 45⟌540 _____

Name: _____

Review

Directions: Estimate the following problems by rounding to the nearest ten, hundred or thousand.

1. 53 x 11 = _____   2. 955 – 538 = _____   3. 96 x 218 = _____

4. 342 + 386 = _____   5. 7,922 ÷ 415 = _____   6. 663 + 774 = _____

7. 6,444 ÷ 37 = _____   8. 533 x 897 = _____   9. 695 – 279 = _____

10. Jerod had 123 cars in his collection. He offered to share them with 6 of his friends. About how many cars should Jerod give each person? _____

11. Emily wanted to buy lunch for herself, her mother and her sister. Each wanted a hamburger at $2.47 each, fries at $0.98 each, a salad at $1.45 each and her sister wanted a milkshake at $1.33. Emily had $16. Did she have enough money to treat everyone? _____

12. Jonathan drove 61 miles on Monday, 23 miles on Tuesday, 46 miles on Wednesday, 72 miles on Thursday and only 9 miles on Friday. Did he drive more or less than 215 miles altogether? _____

13. Brittany collected dolls from all over the world. She had 21 from Spain, 43 from Canada, 65 from England, 24 from the United States and 13 from Japan. She needed 150 to enter in the doll show. Did she have enough? _____

Decimals

A **decimal** is a number that includes a period called a **decimal point**. The digits to the right of the decimal point are a value less than one.

one whole   **one tenth**   **one hundredth**

The place value chart below helps explain decimals.

hundreds	tens	ones		tenths	hundredths	thousandths
6	3	2	.	4		
	4	7	.	0	5	
		8	.	0	0	9

A decimal is read as "and." The first number, 632.4, is read as "six hundred thirty-two and four tenths." The second number, 47.05, is read as "forty-seven and five hundredths." The third number, 8.009, is read as "eight and nine thousandths."

Directions: Write the decimals shown below. Two have been done for you.

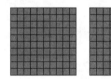

1. __**1.4**__   2. _____   3. _____

4. six and five tenths   __**6.5**__

5. twenty-two and nine tenths   _____

6. thirty-six and fourteen hundredths   _____

7. forty-seven hundredths   _____

8. one hundred six and four tenths   _____

9. seven and three hundredths   _____

10. one tenth less than 0.6   _____

11. one hundredth less than 0.34   _____

12. one tenth more than 0.2   _____

Name: _____

Adding and Subtracting Decimals

When adding or subtracting decimals, place the decimal points under each other. That way, you add tenths to tenths, for example, not tenths to hundredths. Add or subtract beginning on the right, as usual. Carry or borrow numbers in the same way. Adding 0 to the end of decimals does not change their value, but sometimes makes them easier to add and subtract.

Examples:

39.40	0.064	3.56	6.83
+ 6.81	+ 0.470	− .09	− 2.14
46.21	0.534	3.47	4.69

Directions: Solve the following problems.

1. Write each set of numbers in a column and add them.

   a. 2.56 + 0.6 + 76 =   _____

   b. 93.5 + 23.06 + 1.45 =   _____

   c. 3.23 + 91.34 + 0.85 =   _____

2. Write each pair of numbers in a column and subtract them.

   A. 7.89 − 0.56 = _____   B. 34.56 − 6.04 = _____   C. 7.6 − 3.24 = _____

3. In a relay race, Alice ran her part in 23.6 seconds, Cindy did hers in 24.7 seconds and Erin took 20.09 seconds. How many seconds did they take altogether?   _____

4. Although Erin ran her part in 20.09 seconds today, yesterday it took her 21.55 seconds. How much faster was she today?   _____

5. Add this grocery bill:
   potatoes—$3.49; milk—$2.09; bread—$0.99; apples—$2.30   _____

6. A yellow coat cost $47.59, and a blue coat cost $36.79. How much more did the yellow coat cost?   _____

7. A box of Oat Boats cereal has 14.6 ounces. A box of Sugar Circles has 17.85 ounces. How much more cereal is in the Sugar Circles box?   _____

8. The Oat Boats cereal has 4.03 ounces of sugar in it. Sugar Circles cereal has only 3.76 ounces. How much more sugar is in a box of Oats Boats?   _____

Name: _____

Adding and Subtracting Decimals

Directions: Add or subtract the following problems.

1.   53.5
       20.07
    + 1.85

2.   0.05
       0.83
    + 1.04

3.   25.4
       16.09
    + 31.62

4.   16.28
       2.43
    + 11.11

5.   14.29
    − 11.17

6.   48.90
    − 16.49

7.   29.62
    − 19.55

8.   84.13
    − 15.25

9.   4.32
       17.1
      206.06
    + 20.121

10.   1.46
       8.2
       3.003
    + 10.0

11. 146.023
    − 37.105

12. 275.486
    − 75.5

13. The principal organized the creation of a flower garden in front of the school. She purchased 50 daffodils for $23.50, 25 geraniums for $17.75 and 3 rose bushes for $4.00 each. How much did she spend on flowers altogether?

_____

14. In order to complete the project, she would also need topsoil at $10.75 per bag, a shovel at $5.25 each, fertilizer at $3.50 per bag and mulch at $4.15 per bag. She bought two of everything. She only had $100 to spend for this entire project. How much money, if any, did she have left?

_____

Name:_____

Mulitplying Decimals by Two-Digit Numbers

To multiply by a 2-digit number, just repeat the same steps. In the example below, first multiply 4 times 9, 4 times 5 and 4 times 3. Then multiply 2 times 9, 2 times 5 and 2 times 3. You may want to place a 0 in the ones place to make sure this answer, 718, is one digit to the left. Now add 1,436 + 7,180 to get the final answer.

Example:

359	359	359	359	359	359
x 24	x 24	x 24	x 24	x 24	x 24
6	36	1,436	1,436	1,436	1,436
			80	180	7,180
					8,616

When one or both numbers in a multiplication problem have decimals, check to see how many digits are right of the decimal. Then place the decimal the same number of places to the left in the answer. Here's how the example above would change if it included decimals:

35.9	3.59
x 0.24	x 24
8.616	86.16

The first example has one digit to the right of the decimal in 35.9 and two more in 0.24, so the decimal point is placed three digits to the left in the answer: 8.616. The second example has two digits to the right of the decimal in 3.59 and none in 24, so the decimal point is placed two digits to the left in the answer: 86.16. (Notice that you do not have to line up the decimals in a multiplication problem.)

Directions: Solve the following problems.

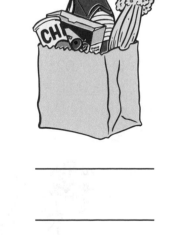

1. Jennie wants to buy 3 T-shirts that cost $15.99 each. How much will they cost altogether?   _____

2. Steve is making $3.75 an hour packing groceries. How much will he make in 8 hours?   _____

3. Justin made 36 cookies and sold them all at the school carnival for $0.75 each. How much money did he make?   _____

4. Last year, the carnival made $467. This year it made 2.3 times as much. How much money did the carnival make this year?   _____

5. Troy's car will go 21.8 miles on a gallon of gasoline. His motorcycle will go 1.7 times as far. How far will his motorcycle travel on one gallon of gas?   _____

Multiplying Decimals With Zeros

The placement of the decimal is the same even if the numbers you're multiplying have zeros in them. As before, count the digits right of the decimal in the numbers you're multiplying and place the decimal the same number of places to the left in the answer.

Examples:

0.87	0.45
x 0.4	x 0.9
0.348	0.405

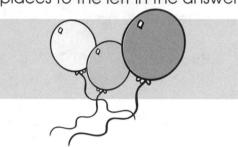

Directions: Solve the following problems.

1. 1.5
    x 0.2

2. 0.67
    x 0.5

3. 1.406
    x   0.5

4. 6.01
    x 1.40

5. 103
    x 0.2

6. 4.0
    x 0.5

7. 1.2
    x 0.05

8. 3.04
    x 0.25

9. 2.05
    x 0.3

10. 4.02
     x 0.7

11. 7.02
     x 0.65

12. 60.9
     x 0.3

13. 80.5
     x 0.2

14. 109
     x 0.5

15. 50
     x 0.25

Name: _____

Multiplying Decimals

In some problems, you may need to add zeros in order to place the decimal point correctly.

Examples:	0.34	0.0067	0.046
	x 0.08	x 4	x 0.07
	0.0272	0.0268	0.00322

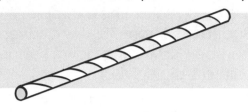

Directions: Solve the following problems.

1.   0.15
x 0.02

2.   0.67
x 0.08

3.   7.3
x 0.06

4.   3.59
x 0.08

5.   0.061
x 0.014

6.   7.10
x 0.042

7.   5.05
x 0.08

8.   8.75
x 0.067

9. 0.0647
x   0.3

10.   3.62
x 0.003

11.   1.07
x 0.05

12.   3.03
x 0.07

13.   0.02
x 0.02

14. 0.501
x 0.03

15. 0.321
x 0.09

16. The players and coaches gathered around for refreshments after the soccer game. Of the 30 people there, 0.50 of them had fruit drinks, 0.20 of them had fruit juice and 0.30 of them had soft drinks. How many people had each type of drink?

fruit drink _____

fruit juice _____

soft drink _____

Name: _____

Dividing Decimals by Two-Digit Numbers

Dividing by a 2-digit divisor (34 in the example below) is very similar to dividing by a 1-digit divisor. In this example, 34 will divide into 78 twice. Then multiply 34 x 2 to get 68. Subtract 68 from 78. The answer is 10, which is smaller than the divisor, so 2 was the right number. Now bring down the next 8. 34 goes into 108 three times. Continue dividing as with a 1-digit divisor.

Example:

$$
\begin{array}{r} 2 \\ 34\overline{)7{,}888} \\ 68 \\ \hline 10 \end{array}
\qquad
\begin{array}{r} 23 \\ 34\overline{)7{,}888} \\ 68 \\ \hline 108 \\ 102 \\ \hline 6 \end{array}
\qquad
\begin{array}{r} 232 \\ 34\overline{)7{,}888} \\ 68 \\ \hline 108 \\ 102 \\ \hline 68 \\ 68 \\ \hline 0 \end{array}
$$

To check your division, multiply: 34 x 232 = 7,888.

When the dividend has a decimal, place the decimal point for the answer directly above the decimal point in the dividend.

Examples:

$$
\begin{array}{r} 3.6 \\ 14\overline{)50.4} \end{array}
\qquad
\begin{array}{r} 8.92 \\ 34\overline{)303.28} \end{array}
$$

Directions: Solve the following problems.

1. $56\overline{)7.28}$
2. $23\overline{)18.63}$
3. $62\overline{)255.44}$
4. $71\overline{)82.36}$
5. $4\overline{)8.580}$

6. If socks cost $8.97 for 3 pairs, how much does one pair cost? _____

7. If candy bars are 6 for $2.58, how much is one candy bar? _____

8. You buy a bike for $152.25 and agree to make 21 equal payments. How much will each payment be? _____

9. You and two friends agree to spend several hours loading a truck. The truck driver gives you $36.75 to share. How much will each person get? _____

10. You buy 14 hamburgers and the bill comes to $32.06. How much did each hamburger cost? _____

Working With Decimals

Directions: Solve the following problems.

1. 0.79 x 3.2	2. 840 x 0.25	3. 6.53 x 0.06	4. 0.724 x 0.04	5. 1.92 x 2.3

6. $6\overline{)21.6}$ 7. $4\overline{)9.36}$ 8. $50\overline{)630.50}$ 9. $25\overline{)60.50}$ 10. $55\overline{)44.55}$

11. Ice-cream cones are on special at $1.29 for a double scoop. If you buy 3 of them, how much will you need to pay? _____

12. Each cone has 2.5 ounces of ice cream on it. How much ice cream is needed to serve 100 cones? _____

13. If ice cream sells for $10.25 for 1 gallon, how much would 0.5 gallon cost? _____

14. The ice-cream shop sells approximately 1,500 cones per week. How many does it sell in one day? _____

Name: _____

Dividing With Zeros

Sometimes you have a remainder in division problems. You can add a decimal point and zeros to the dividend and keep dividing until you have the answer.

Example:

$$
\begin{array}{r}
49 \\
25\,\overline{)1{,}241} \\
1\,00 \\
\hline
241 \\
225 \\
\hline
16
\end{array}
\qquad
\begin{array}{r}
49.64 \\
25\,\overline{)1{,}241.00} \\
1\,00 \\
\hline
241 \\
225 \\
\hline
160 \\
150 \\
\hline
100 \\
100 \\
\hline
0
\end{array}
$$

Directions: Solve the following problems.

1. $2\overline{)2.5}$ 2. $4\overline{)115}$ 3. $12\overline{)738}$ 4. $8\overline{)586}$ 5. $25\overline{)3{,}415}$

6. Susie's grandparents sent her a check for $130 to share with her 7 brothers and sisters. How much will each of the 8 children get if the money is divided evenly?   _____

7. A vendor had 396 balloons to sell and 16 workers. How many balloons should each worker sell in order to sell out?   _____

8. Eight of the workers turned in a total of $753. How much did each worker collect if he/she sold the same number of items?   _____

9. A total of 744 tickets were collected from 15 amusement ride operators on the first day of the fair. If each ride required one ticket per person, and they each collected the same number of tickets, how many people rode each ride?   _____

   Do you think that was possible? Why? _____

   _____

10. Five people were hired to clean up the area after the fair closed. They turned in a bill for 26 hours of labor. How many hours did each person work?   _____

Name:_____

Dividing With Zeros

Sometimes you need a zero to hold a place in the answer. In the first example below, 7 goes into 21 three times. But 7 can't be divided into 2, the next number in the dividend, so place a 0 above the 2 in the dividend. Then bring down the next number in the dividend, 8, and continue dividing.

Examples:

$$\begin{array}{r} 304 \\ 7\overline{)2{,}128} \\ 21 \\ \hline 028 \\ 28 \\ \hline 0 \end{array}$$

$$\begin{array}{r} 106 \\ 6\overline{)636} \\ 6 \\ \hline 036 \\ 36 \\ \hline 0 \end{array}$$

$$\begin{array}{r} 200.5 \\ 4\overline{)802.0} \\ 8 \\ \hline 0020 \\ 20 \\ \hline 0 \end{array}$$

Directions: Solve the following problems, adding zeros where necessary. Check each answer by multiplying the divisor by the answer to get the dividend.

1. $5\overline{)251}$ 2. $16\overline{)324}$ 3. $8\overline{)2{,}448}$ 4. $8\overline{)326}$ 5. $57\overline{)51{,}528}$

6. $7\overline{)1{,}435}$ 7. $4\overline{)1{,}015}$ 8. $5\overline{)5{,}020}$ 9. $25\overline{)16{,}064}$ 10. $60\overline{)24{,}030}$

11. Jimmy had 155 small pieces of candy to share with 4 of his friends. If they divide the candy evenly among the 5 children, how much will each child get?   _____

12. For an art project, 5 boys divided up 530 beads. How many beads did they each get?   _____

13. If 8 packs of gum cost $8.48, how much did each pack cost?   _____

Name:_____

Dividing Decimals by Decimals

When a divisor has a decimal, eliminate it before dividing. If there is one digit right of the decimal in the divisor, multiply the divisor and dividend by 10. If there are two digits right of the decimal in the divisor, multiply the divisor and dividend by 100.

Multiply the divisor and dividend by the same number whether or not the dividend has a decimal. The goal is to have a divisor with no decimal.

Examples: $2.3\overline{)89}$ x 10 = $23\overline{)890}$ $4.11\overline{)67.7}$ x 100 = $411\overline{)6{,}770}$

$4.9\overline{)35.67}$ x 10 = $49\overline{)356.7}$ $0.34\overline{)789}$ x 100 = $34\overline{)78{,}900}$

After removing the decimal from the divisor, work the problem in the usual way.

Directions: Solve the following problems.

1. $3.5\overline{)10.15}$ 2. $6.7\overline{)415.4}$ 3. $0.21\overline{)924}$ 4. $73\overline{)50.37}$

5. The body can burn only 0.00015 of an ounce of alcohol an hour. If an average-sized person has 1 drink, his/her blood alcohol concentration (BAC) is 0.0003. How many hours will it take his/her body to remove that much alcohol from the blood?   _____

6. If the same person has 2 drinks in 1 hour, his/her blood alcohol concentration increases to 0.0006. Burning 0.00015 ounce of alcohol an hour, how many hours will it take that person's body to burn off 2 drinks?   _____

7. If someone has 3 drinks in 1 hour, the blood alcohol concentration rises to 0.0009. At 0.00015 an hour, how many hours will it take to burn off 3 drinks?   _____

8. After a drunk driving conviction, the driver's car insurance can increase by as much as $2,000. Still, this is only 0.57 of the total cost of the conviction. What is the total cost, in round numbers?   _____

9. In Ohio in 1986, about 335 fatal car crashes were alcohol related. That was 0.47 of the total number of fatal car crashes. About how many crashes were there altogether, in round numbers?   _____

Name: _____

Review

Directions: Solve the following problems.

1. Write these numbers as decimals:

   a. thirty-six and seventy-four hundredths   _____

   b. twenty-nine and four tenths   _____

   c. sixty-five hundredths   _____

   d. one tenth less than 0.7   _____

2. Blue Bridge is 0.45 miles long, while Yellow Bridge is 1.23 miles long. How much longer is Yellow Bridge than Blue Bridge?   _____

3. Chris spent 23.6 minutes studying for a history test, 17.54 minutes doing math problems and 19.4 minutes writing a short story. How many minutes did Chris spend on homework altogether?   _____

4. Sean's truck can carry 1,289.5 pounds. How many pounds would it hold if it were 0.75 full?   _____

5. Sherri has a picture that is 3.5 inches wide. She plans to enlarge it 2.5 times. How wide would it be then?   _____

6. A computer printer takes 0.025 of a second to print one letter. How long would it take to print the word *technology*?   _____

7. Statistics show that 0.97 of the 6,500,000 alcoholics in the U.S. are ordinary people, not "bums," as some think. How many alcoholics in the U.S. are ordinary people?   _____

8. At Super Store, a package of blank tapes costs $5.96 for 4 tapes. Sav-Here sells a package of 6 tapes for $7.20. How much could you save on each blank tape at Sav-Here?   _____

9. If you wanted to divide 8.5 pounds of sugar equally into 4 bowls, exactly how many pounds should you place in each bowl?   _____

10. Ten workers picked 832 oranges in 8 minutes. How many did they all pick every minute, on average?   _____

Review

Directions: Follow the instructions below.

Add.

1. 5.23	2. 49.40	3. 92.5	4. 81.45
+ 6.07	+ 3.81	+ 7.45	2.37
			+ 5.10

5. Brian bought the following items: shoes for $79.00, jeans for $45.50
   and a hat for $17.95. How much did he spend altogether?   _____

Subtract.

1. 5.6	2. 24.36	3. 87.68	4. 1.03
− 2.34	− 6.07	− 46.70	− 0.97

5. Liz used a $20 bill for a purchase of $14.98. How much change
   should she get back?   _____

Multiply.

1. 4.82	2. 61.08	3. 15.3	4. 145.06
x 34	x 1.5	x 2.7	x 0.43

5. Greg bought 3 soccer balls for $47.50 each. How much did he
   spend altogether?   _____

Divide.

1. $4\overline{)52.6}$ 2. $18\overline{)93.6}$ 3. $45\overline{)5.13}$ 4. $40\overline{)70.6}$

5. Krysti selected 12 CD's at the music store, all at the same cost.
   Her total bill was $87. How much did she pay for each CD?   _____

Decimals and Fractions

A **fraction** is a number that names part of something. The top number in a fraction is called the **numerator**. The bottom number is called the **denominator**. Since a decimal also names part of a whole number, every decimal can also be written as a fraction. For example, 0.1 is read as "one tenth" and can also be written $\frac{1}{10}$. The decimal 0.56 is read as "fifty-six hundredths" and can also be written $\frac{56}{100}$.

Examples:

$$0.7 = \frac{7}{10} \qquad 0.34 = \frac{34}{100} \qquad 0.761 = \frac{761}{1,000} \qquad \frac{5}{10} = 0.5 \qquad \frac{58}{100} = 0.58 \qquad \frac{729}{1,000} = 0.729$$

Even a fraction that doesn't have 10, 100 or 1,000 as the denominator can be written as a decimal. Sometimes you can multiply both the numerator and denominator by a certain number so the denominator is 10, 100 or 1,000. (You can't just multiply the denominator. That would change the amount of the fraction.)

Examples:

$$\frac{3 \times 2}{5 \times 2} = \frac{6}{10} = 0.6 \qquad\qquad \frac{4 \times 4}{25 \times 4} = \frac{16}{100} = 0.16$$

Other times, divide the numerator by the denominator.

Examples:

$$\frac{3}{4} = 4\overline{)3.00} = 0.75 \qquad\qquad \frac{5}{8} = 8\overline{)5.000} = 0.625$$

Directions: Follow the instructions below.

1. For each square, write a decimal and a fraction to show the part that is colored. The first one has been done for you.

   a. 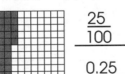 $\frac{25}{100}$

   0.25

   b. 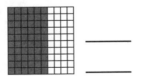 _____

   _____

   c. 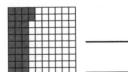 _____

   _____

2. Change these decimals to fractions.

   a. 0.6 =   b. 0.54 =   c. 0.751 =   d. 0.73 =   e. 0.592 =   f. 0.2 =

3. Change these fractions to decimals. If necessary, round off the decimals to the nearest hundredth.

   a. $\frac{3}{10} =$ b. $\frac{89}{100} =$ c. $\frac{473}{1,000} =$ d. $\frac{4}{5} =$ e. $\frac{35}{50} =$

   f. $\frac{7}{9} =$ g. $\frac{1}{3} =$ h. $\frac{23}{77} =$ i. $\frac{12}{63} =$ j. $\frac{4}{16} =$

Name: _____

Equivalent Fractions and the Lowest Term

Equivalent fractions name the same amount. For example, $\frac{1}{2}$, $\frac{5}{10}$, and $\frac{50}{100}$ are exactly the same amount. They all mean half of something. (And they are all written as the same decimal: 0.5.) To find an equivalent fraction, multiply the numerator and denominator of any fraction by the same number.

Examples: $\frac{3 \times 3 = 9 \times 4 = 36}{4 \times 3 = 12 \times 4 = 48}$ Thus, $\frac{3}{4}$, $\frac{9}{12}$ and $\frac{36}{48}$ are all equivalent fractions.

Most of the time, we want fractions in their lowest terms. It's easier to work with $\frac{3}{4}$ than $\frac{36}{48}$. To find a fraction's lowest term, instead of multiplying both parts of a fraction by the same number, divide.

Examples: $\frac{36 \div 12 = 3}{48 \div 12 = 4}$ The lowest term for $\frac{36}{48}$ is $\frac{3}{4}$.

If the numerator and denominator in a fraction can't be divided by any number, the fraction is in its lowest term. The fractions below are in their lowest terms.

Examples: $\frac{34}{61}$ $\frac{3}{5}$ $\frac{7}{9}$ $\frac{53}{90}$ $\frac{78}{83}$ $\frac{3}{8}$

Directions: Follow the instructions below.

1. Write two equivalent fractions for each fraction. Make sure you multiply the numerator and denominator by the same number. The first one is done for you.

   a. $\frac{1 \times 3 = 3}{2 \times 3 = 6}$ $\frac{1 \times 4 = 4}{2 \times 4 = 8}$

   b. $\frac{2 \times \underline{\quad} = \underline{\quad}}{3 \times \underline{\quad} = \underline{\quad}}$ $\frac{2 \times \underline{\quad} = \underline{\quad}}{3 \times \underline{\quad} = \underline{\quad}}$

   c. $\frac{3 \times \underline{\quad} = \underline{\quad}}{5 \times \underline{\quad} = \underline{\quad}}$ $\frac{3 \times \underline{\quad} = \underline{\quad}}{5 \times \underline{\quad} = \underline{\quad}}$

   d. $\frac{8 \times \underline{\quad} = \underline{\quad}}{9 \times \underline{\quad} = \underline{\quad}}$ $\frac{8 \times \underline{\quad} = \underline{\quad}}{9 \times \underline{\quad} = \underline{\quad}}$

2. Find the lowest terms for each fraction. Make sure your answers can't be divided by any other numbers. The first one has been done for you.

   a. $\frac{2 \div 2 = 1}{36 \div 2 = 18}$

   b. $\frac{12 \div \underline{\quad} = \underline{\quad}}{25 \div \underline{\quad} = \underline{\quad}}$

   c. $\frac{12 \div \underline{\quad} = \underline{\quad}}{16 \div \underline{\quad} = \underline{\quad}}$

   d. $\frac{3 \div \underline{\quad} = \underline{\quad}}{9 \div \underline{\quad} = \underline{\quad}}$

   e. $\frac{25 \div \underline{\quad} = \underline{\quad}}{45 \div \underline{\quad} = \underline{\quad}}$

   f. $\frac{11 \div \underline{\quad} = \underline{\quad}}{44 \div \underline{\quad} = \underline{\quad}}$

Greatest Common Factor

The **greatest common factor (GCF)** is the largest number that will divide evenly into a set of numbers. In the example, both numbers can be divided evenly by 2 and 4; therefore, 4 is the greatest common factor.

Example: 12 and 20   2, 4 (can be divided evenly into both numbers)
4 (greatest common factor)

Directions: Circle the greatest common factor for each pair of numbers.

1. 56 and 72	6	10	8	2
2. 45 and 81	7	5	9	3
3. 28 and 49	7	11	4	6
4. 10 and 35	3	5	9	7
5. 42 and 30	4	2	5	6
6. 121 and 33	12	9	4	11
7. 96 and 48	48	15	6	3
8. 12 and 132	2	10	12	9
9. 108 and 27	14	9	3	27
10. 44 and 32	4	6	8	10
11. 16 and 88	12	2	8	5
12. 72 and 144	9	11	7	72

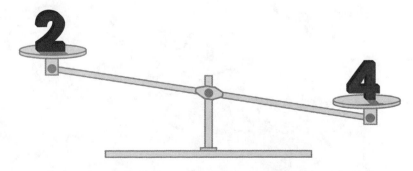

43

Least Common Multiple

The **least common multiple (LCM)** is the lowest possible multiple any pair of numbers have in common.

Examples: 2 and 4
The lowest common multiple is 4, because 4 is a multiple for each number and it is the lowest possible.

6 and 7
Multiples of 6 are 6, 12, 18, 24, 30, 36, 42.
Multiples of 7 are 7, 14, 21, 28, 35, 42.
42 is the lowest multiple that 6 and 7 have in common.

Directions: Find the least common multiple for each pair of numbers.

1. 7 and 8 = _____

2. 2 and 3 = _____

3. 11 and 4 = _____

4. 5 and 3 = _____

5. 7 and 2 = _____

6. 9 and 4 = _____

7. 2 and 6 = _____

8. 10 and 3 = _____

9. 7 and 5 = _____

10. 9 and 6 = _____

11. 12 and 8 = _____

12. 15 and 3 = _____

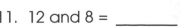

Comparing Decimals and Fractions

The symbol **>** means greater than. The number on its left is greater than that on its right. The symbol **<** means less than. The number on its left is less than that on its right. An equal sign, **=**, shows the same value on each side.

Directions: Use the sign >, = or < to make each statement true.

1. 0.4 ◯ $\frac{2}{3}$ 2. 1.25 ◯ $\frac{3}{2}$

3. 0.7 ◯ $\frac{4}{5}$ 4. 0.68 ◯ $\frac{5}{7}$

5. 0.1 ◯ $\frac{1}{12}$ 6. 0.45 ◯ $\frac{1}{2}$

7. 0.75 ◯ $\frac{3}{8}$ 8. 0.6 ◯ $\frac{5}{8}$

9. 0.54 ◯ $\frac{2}{5}$ 10. 0.8 ◯ $\frac{4}{6}$

11. 0.25 ◯ $\frac{1}{7}$ 12. 1.8 ◯ $\frac{12}{7}$

13. 0.625 ◯ $\frac{4}{8}$ 14. 0.33 ◯ $\frac{1}{3}$

15. Jenna looked carefully at the labels on two different types of cookies. The chocolate ones had $\frac{3}{4}$ pound in the package. The package of vanilla cookies claimed it had 0.67 pound of cookies inside. Were the chocolate cookies <, > or = to the vanilla cookies? _____

Name: _____

Mixed Numbers and Improper Fractions

A **mixed number** is a whole number and a fraction, such as $1\frac{3}{4}$. An **improper fraction** has a numerator that is larger than its denominator, such as $\frac{16}{3}$. To write an improper fraction as a mixed number, divide the numerator by the denominator. The quotient becomes the whole number and the remainder becomes the fraction.

Examples:

$$\frac{16}{3} = 3\overline{)16} = 5\frac{1}{3}$$
$$\frac{15}{1}$$

$$\frac{28}{5} = 5\overline{)28} = 5\frac{3}{5}$$
$$\frac{25}{3}$$

To change a mixed number into an improper fraction, multiply the whole number by the denominator and add the numerator.

Examples: $4\frac{1}{3} = 4 \times 3 = 12 + 1 = 13 \quad \frac{13}{3}$

$8\frac{4}{7} = 8 \times 7 = 56 + 4 = 60 \quad \frac{60}{7}$

Directions: Follow the instructions below.

1. Change the improper fractions to mixed numbers and reduce to lowest terms. Use another sheet of paper if necessary. The first one has been done for you.

   a. $\frac{34}{6} = 6\overline{)34} = 5\frac{4}{6} = 5\frac{2}{3}$
   $$\frac{30}{4}$$

   b. $\frac{65}{4} =$ _____

   c. $\frac{23}{8} =$ _____

   d. $\frac{89}{3} =$ _____

   e. $\frac{45}{9} =$ _____

   f. $\frac{32}{5} =$ _____

   g. $\frac{13}{7} =$ _____

   h. $\frac{24}{9} =$ _____

   i. $\frac{31}{2} =$ _____

   j. $\frac{84}{23} =$ _____

2. Change these mixed numbers into improper fractions. The first one has been done for you.

   a. $4\frac{6}{7} = 4 \times 7 = 28 + 6 = \frac{34}{7}$

   b. $2\frac{1}{9} =$ ——

   c. $5\frac{4}{5} =$ ——

   d. $12\frac{1}{4} =$ ——

   e. $6\frac{7}{8} =$ ——

   f. $3\frac{9}{11} =$ ——

   g. $8\frac{3}{12} =$ ——

   h. $1\frac{6}{14} =$ ——

   i. $4\frac{2}{3} =$ ——

   j. $9\frac{4}{15} =$ ——

Name: _____

Review

Directions: Match the following mixed numbers with the equivalent improper fractions.

1. $\dfrac{25}{4}$ = _____

2. $\dfrac{32}{6}$ = _____

3. $\dfrac{17}{2}$ = _____

4. $\dfrac{84}{9}$ = _____

5. $\dfrac{67}{5}$ = _____

6. $\dfrac{94}{8}$ = _____

7. $\dfrac{48}{5}$ = _____

8. $\dfrac{99}{12}$ = _____

9. $\dfrac{57}{6}$ = _____

10. $\dfrac{65}{7}$ = _____

11. $\dfrac{87}{15}$ = _____

12. $\dfrac{34}{4}$ = _____

13. $\dfrac{53}{2}$ = _____

14. $\dfrac{82}{5}$ = _____

15. $\dfrac{78}{9}$ = _____

A. $13\dfrac{2}{5}$

B. $9\dfrac{1}{2}$

C. $8\dfrac{1}{2}$

D. $6\dfrac{1}{4}$

E. $26\dfrac{1}{2}$

F. $9\dfrac{2}{7}$

G. $5\dfrac{1}{3}$

H. $8\dfrac{1}{2}$

I. $16\dfrac{2}{5}$

J. $8\dfrac{1}{4}$

K. $9\dfrac{3}{5}$

L. $11\dfrac{3}{4}$

M. $9\dfrac{1}{3}$

N. $5\dfrac{4}{5}$

O. $8\dfrac{2}{3}$

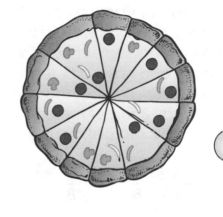

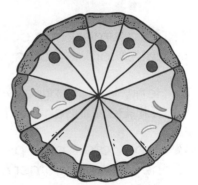

Name: _____

Adding Fractions

When adding fractions, if the denominators are the same, simply add the numerators. When the result is an improper fraction, change it to a mixed number.

Examples: $\dfrac{3}{5} + \dfrac{1}{5} = \dfrac{4}{5}$ $\dfrac{3}{9} + \dfrac{7}{9} = \dfrac{10}{9} = 1\dfrac{1}{9}$

If the denominators of fractions are different, change them so they are the same. To do this, find equivalent fractions. In the first example below, $\frac{1}{4}$ and $\frac{3}{8}$ have different denominators, so change $\frac{1}{4}$ to the equivalent fraction $\frac{2}{8}$. Then add the numerators. In the second example, $\frac{5}{7}$ and $\frac{2}{3}$ also have different denominators. Find a denominator both 7 and 3 divide into. The lowest number they both divide into is 21. Multiply the numerator and denominator of $\frac{5}{7}$ by 3 to get the equivalent fraction $\frac{15}{21}$. Then multiply the numerator and denominator of $\frac{2}{3}$ by 7 to get the equivalent fraction $\frac{14}{21}$.

Examples:

$$\dfrac{1 \times 2 = 2}{4 \times 2 = 8}$$
$$\dfrac{3}{8}$$
$$+\dfrac{3}{8}$$

$$\dfrac{2}{8}$$
$$\dfrac{3}{8}$$
$$+\dfrac{3}{8}$$
$$\dfrac{5}{8}$$

$$\dfrac{5 \times 3 = 15}{7 \times 3 = 21}$$
$$\dfrac{2 \times 7 = 14}{+ \ 3 \times 7 = 21}$$
$$\dfrac{29}{21} = 1\dfrac{8}{21}$$

Directions: Solve the following problems. Find equivalent fractions when necessary.

1. $\dfrac{3}{5}$
    $\dfrac{1}{5}$
    $+\dfrac{}{}$

2. $\dfrac{7}{8}$
    $\dfrac{2}{16}$
    $+\dfrac{}{}$

3. $\dfrac{1}{9}$
    $\dfrac{2}{3}$
    $+\dfrac{}{}$

4. $\dfrac{2}{6}$
    $\dfrac{2}{3}$
    $+\dfrac{}{}$

5. $\dfrac{2}{15}$
    $\dfrac{1}{5}$
    $+\dfrac{}{}$

6. Cora is making a cake. She needs $\frac{1}{2}$ cup butter for the cake and $\frac{1}{4}$ cup butter for the frosting. How much butter does she need altogether? _____

7. Henry is painting a wall. Yesterday he painted $\frac{1}{3}$ of it. Today he painted $\frac{1}{4}$ of it. How much has he painted altogether?

8. Nancy ate $\frac{1}{6}$ of a pie. Her father ate $\frac{1}{4}$ of it. How much did they eat altogether? _____

Name:_____

Subtracting Fractions

Subtracting fractions is very similar to adding them in that the denominators must be the same. If the denominators are different, use equivalent fractions.

Examples:

$$\begin{array}{r} \frac{3}{4} \\ -\frac{1}{4} \\ \hline \frac{2}{4} = \frac{1}{2} \end{array}$$

$$\begin{array}{r} 2 \times 8 = \frac{16}{40} \\ 5 \times 8 \\ 1 \times 5 = \frac{5}{40} \\ -8 \times 5 \\ \hline \frac{11}{40} \end{array}$$

Adding and subtracting mixed numbers are also similar. Often, though, change the mixed numbers to improper fractions. If the denominators are different, use equivalent fractions.

Examples:

$$\begin{array}{r} 2\frac{3}{5} = \frac{13}{5} \\ -1\frac{4}{5} = \frac{9}{5} \\ \hline \frac{4}{5} \end{array}$$

$$\begin{array}{r} 3\frac{3}{14} = \frac{45}{14} \qquad = \frac{45}{14} \\ -2\frac{1}{7} = \frac{15 \times 2}{7 \times 2} = \frac{30}{14} \\ \hline \frac{15}{14} = 1\frac{1}{14} \end{array}$$

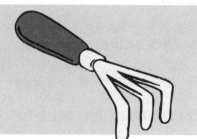

Directions: Solve the following problems. Use equivalent fractions and improper fractions where necessary.

1. $\begin{array}{r} \frac{6}{7} \\ -\frac{5}{7} \\ \hline \end{array}$

2. $\begin{array}{r} 1\frac{2}{9} \\ -\frac{4}{9} \\ \hline \end{array}$

3. $\begin{array}{r} 2\frac{3}{6} \\ -\frac{4}{5} \\ \hline \end{array}$

4. $\begin{array}{r} \frac{3}{4} \\ -\frac{1}{2} \\ \hline \end{array}$

5. $\begin{array}{r} 2\frac{1}{3} \\ -\frac{3}{4} \\ \hline \end{array}$

6. Carol promised to weed the flower garden for $1\frac{1}{2}$ hours this morning. So far she has pulled two weeds for $\frac{3}{4}$ of an hour. How much longer does she have to work?

_____

7. Dil started out with $1\frac{1}{4}$ gallons of paint. He used $\frac{3}{8}$ of the paint on his boat. How much paint is left?

_____

8. A certain movie lasts $2\frac{1}{2}$ hours. Susan has already watched it for $1\frac{2}{3}$ hours. How much longer is the movie?

_____

9. Bert didn't finish $\frac{1}{8}$ of the math problems on a test. He made mistakes on $\frac{1}{6}$ of the problems. The rest he answered correctly. What fraction of the problems did he answer correctly?

_____

Multiplying Fractions

To multiply two fractions, multiply the numerators and then multiply the denominators. If necessary, change the answer to its lowest term.

Examples: $\dfrac{3}{4} \times \dfrac{2}{3} = \dfrac{6}{12} = \dfrac{1}{2}$ $\dfrac{1}{8} \times \dfrac{4}{5} = \dfrac{4}{40} = \dfrac{1}{10}$

To multiply a whole number by a fraction, first write the whole number as a fraction (with 1 as the denominator). Then multiply as above. You may need to change an improper fraction to a mixed number.

Examples: $\dfrac{2}{3} \times \dfrac{4}{1} = \dfrac{8}{3} = 2\dfrac{2}{3}$ $\dfrac{3}{7} \times \dfrac{6}{1} = \dfrac{18}{7} = 2\dfrac{4}{7}$

Directions: Solve the following problems, writing answers in their lowest terms.

1. $\dfrac{1}{5} \times \dfrac{2}{3} =$ 2. $\dfrac{1}{3} \times \dfrac{4}{7} =$ 3. $\dfrac{2}{8} \times 3 =$ 4. $\dfrac{2}{6} \times \dfrac{1}{2} =$

5. Tim lost $\frac{1}{8}$ of his marbles. If he had 56 marbles, how many did he lose? _____

6. Jeff is making $\frac{2}{3}$ of a recipe for spaghetti sauce. How much will he need of each ingredient below? _____

   $1\frac{1}{4}$ cups water = _____   2 cups tomato paste = _____

   $\frac{3}{4}$ teaspoon oregano = _____ $4\frac{1}{2}$ teaspoons salt = _____

7. Carrie bought 2 dozen donuts and asked for $\frac{3}{4}$ of them to be chocolate. How many were chocolate? _____

8. Christy let her hair grow 14 inches long and then had $\frac{1}{4}$ of it cut off. How much was cut off? _____

9. Kurt has finished $\frac{7}{8}$ of 40 math problems. How many has he done? _____

10. If Sherryl's cat eats $\frac{2}{3}$ can of cat food every day, how many cans should Sherryl buy for a week? _____

Name:_____

Dividing Fractions

Reciprocals are two fractions that, when multiplied together, make 1. To divide a fraction by a fraction, turn one of the fractions upside down and multiply. The upside-down fraction is a reciprocal of its original fraction. If you multiply a fraction by its reciprocal, you always get 1.

Examples of reciprocals: $\frac{2}{3} \times \frac{3}{2} = \frac{6}{6} = 1$ $\qquad$ $\frac{9}{11} \times \frac{11}{9} = \frac{99}{99} = 1$

Examples of dividing by fractions: $\frac{1}{2} \div \frac{2}{3} = \frac{1}{2} \times \frac{3}{2} = \frac{3}{4}$ $\qquad$ $\frac{2}{5} \div \frac{2}{7} = \frac{2}{5} \times \frac{7}{2} = \frac{14}{10} = \frac{7}{5} = 1\frac{2}{5}$

To divide a whole number by a fraction, first write the whole number as a fraction (with a denominator of 1). (Write a mixed number as an improper fraction.) Then finish the problem as explained above.

Examples: $4 \div \frac{2}{6} = \frac{4}{1} \times \frac{6}{2} = \frac{24}{2} = 12$ $\qquad$ $3\frac{1}{2} \div \frac{2}{5} = \frac{7}{2} \times \frac{5}{2} = \frac{35}{4} = 8\frac{3}{4}$

Directions: Solve the following problems, writing answers in their lowest terms. Change any improper fractions to mixed numbers.

1. $\frac{1}{3} \div \frac{2}{5} =$ $\qquad$ 2. $\frac{6}{7} \div \frac{1}{3} =$ $\qquad$ 3. $3 \div \frac{3}{4} =$ $\qquad$ 4. $\frac{1}{4} \div \frac{2}{3} =$

5. Judy has 8 candy bars. She wants to give $\frac{1}{3}$ of a candy bar to everyone in her class. Does she have enough for all 24 students? _____

6. A big jar of glue holds $3\frac{1}{2}$ cups. How many little containers that hold $\frac{1}{4}$ cup each can you fill? _____

7. A container holds 27 ounces of ice cream. How many $4\frac{1}{2}$-ounce servings is that? _____

8. It takes $2\frac{1}{2}$ teaspoons of powdered mix to make 1 cup of hot chocolate. How many cups can you make with 45 teaspoons of mix? _____

9. Each cup of hot chocolate also takes $\frac{2}{3}$ cup of milk. How many cups of hot chocolate can you make with 12 cups of milk? _____

Name:_____

Review

Directions: Follow the instructions below.

1. Write each of these decimals as fractions

   a. 0.43 =   b. 0.6 =   c. 0.783 =   d. 0.91 =

2. Write each of these fractions as decimals, rounding them off to the nearest hundredth

   a. $\frac{3}{10}$ =   b. $\frac{4}{7}$ =   c. $\frac{3}{9}$ =   d. $\frac{64}{100}$ =

3. Write two equivalent fractions for each of these

   a. $\frac{2}{6}$ =   b. $\frac{1}{4}$ =   c. $\frac{5}{8}$ =

4. Change these fractions into their lowest terms

   a. $\frac{4}{16}$ =   b. $\frac{6}{18}$ =   c. $\frac{5}{90}$ =   d. $\frac{9}{24}$ =

5. Change these improper fractions into mixed numbers

   a. $\frac{30}{9}$ =   b. $\frac{46}{3}$ =   c. $\frac{38}{6}$ =   d. $\frac{18}{4}$ =

6. Change these mixed numbers into improper fractions

   a. $3\frac{1}{6}$ =   b. $7\frac{3}{8}$ =   c. $4\frac{2}{7}$ =   d. $8\frac{1}{9}$ =

7. George has written $1\frac{1}{8}$ pages of a report that is supposed to be $3\frac{1}{2}$ pages long. How much more does he have to write?   _____

8. Jackie ate $\frac{3}{8}$ of half a cake. How much of the whole cake did she eat?   _____

9. Connie's family is driving to Los Angeles. They drove $\frac{1}{6}$ of the way the first day and $\frac{1}{5}$ of the way the second day. How much of the trip have they completed so far?   _____

10. Kenny gets $6 a week for his allowance. He saved $\frac{1}{2}$ of it last week and $\frac{1}{3}$ of it this week. How much money did he save in these 2 weeks?   _____

11. Of 32 students in one class, $\frac{5}{8}$ have a brother or sister. How many students are only children?   _____

12. In one class, $\frac{1}{5}$ of the students were born in January, $\frac{1}{10}$ in February and $\frac{1}{10}$ in March. How much of the class was born in these 3 months?   _____

Name: _____

Review

Directions: Follow the instructions below.

Add.

1. $\dfrac{4}{16} + \dfrac{5}{8} =$ 2. $\dfrac{1}{6} + \dfrac{1}{3} =$ 3. $\dfrac{2}{10} + \dfrac{4}{5} =$ 4. $\dfrac{3}{5} + \dfrac{9}{10} =$

Subtract.

1. $\dfrac{15}{9} - \dfrac{2}{3} =$ 2. $\dfrac{3}{4} - \dfrac{3}{8} =$ 3. $\dfrac{4}{7} - \dfrac{2}{14} =$ 4. $\dfrac{3}{5} - \dfrac{1}{10} =$

Multiply.

1. $\dfrac{1}{2} \times \dfrac{4}{16} =$ 2. $\dfrac{1}{3} \times \dfrac{4}{9} =$ 3. $\dfrac{5}{12} \times \dfrac{1}{4} =$ 4. $\dfrac{3}{16} \times \dfrac{3}{4} =$

Divide.

1. $\dfrac{3}{5} \div \dfrac{1}{3} =$ 2. $4 \div \dfrac{1}{2} =$ 3. $\dfrac{1}{4} \div \dfrac{1}{3} =$ 4. $3\dfrac{3}{4} \div \dfrac{1}{3} =$

Write >, < or = to make the statements true.

1. 0.5 ◯ $\dfrac{5}{8}$ 2. 0.8 ◯ $\dfrac{4}{5}$ 3. 0.35 ◯ $\dfrac{2}{5}$ 4. 1.3 ◯ $\dfrac{7}{8}$

Name: _____

Perimeter

The **perimeter** is the distance around a shape formed by straight lines, such as a square or triangle. To find the perimeter of a shape, add the lengths of its sides.

Examples:

8 in.

8 in. [square]

5 in.

4 in. [rectangle]

3 in.  5 in.

4 in.

For the square, add 8 + 8 + 8 + 8 = 32. Or, write a formula using **P** for **perimeter** and **s** for the **sides**:   P = 4 x s
P = 4 x 8
P = 32 inches

For the rectangle, add 4 + 5 + 4 + 5 = 18. Or, use a different formula, using **l** for **length** and **w** for **width**. In formulas with parentheses, first do the adding, multiplying, and so on, in the parentheses.:

P = (2 x l) + (2 x w)
P = (2 x 5) + (2 x 4)
P = 10 + 8
P = 18

For the triangle, the sides are all different lengths, so the formula doesn't help. Instead, add the sides: 3 + 4 + 5 = 12 inches.

Directions: Find the perimeter of each shape below. Use the formula whenever possible.

10 ft.

8 ft.

6 ft.

11 ft.

3 ft.

4 ft.

1. Find the perimeter of the room pictured at left.   P = _____

2. Brandy plans to frame a picture with a sheet of construction paper. Her picture is 8 in. wide and 13 in. long. She wants the frame to extend 1 in. beyond the picture on all sides. How wide and long should the frame be? What is the perimeter of her picture and of the frame?

Length and width of frame: _____

Perimeter of picture: _____

Perimeter of frame: _____

3. A square has a perimeter of 120 feet. How long is each side?   _____

4. A triangle with equal sides has a perimeter of 96 inches. How long is each side?   _____

5. A rectangle has two sides that are each 14 feet long and a perimeter of 50 feet. How wide is it?   _____

Name: _____

Perimeter

Directions: Find the perimeter of each shape below.

1.

P = _____

2.

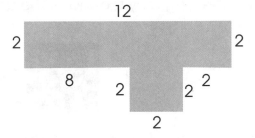

P = _____

3.

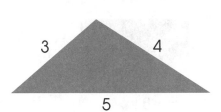

P = _____

4.

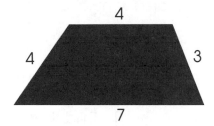

P = _____

5.

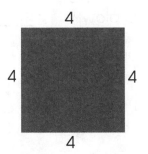

P = _____

6.

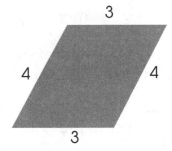

P = _____

7.

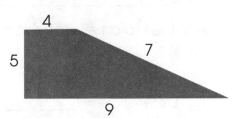

P = _____

8.

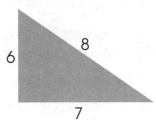

P = _____

Name: _____

Area: Squares and Rectangles

The **area** is the number of square units that covers a certain space. To find the area, multiply the length by the width. The answer is in square units, shown by adding a superscript 2 (^{2}) to the number.

Examples: 3 in.

 5 in.

For the rectangle, use this formula: **A = l x w**
8 in.
A = 8 x 5
A = 40 in.^{2}

For the square formula, **s** stands for side: **A = s x s** (or s^2)
A = 3 x 3 (or 3^2)
A = 9 in.^{2}

Directions: Find the area of each shape below.

7 ft.

 12 ft.

1. Find the area of a room which is 12 feet long and 7 feet wide.   A = _____

2. A farmer's field is 32 feet on each side. How many square feet does he have to plow?   _____

3. Steve's bedroom is 10 feet by 12 feet. How many square feet of carpeting would cover the floor?   _____

4. Two of Steve's walls are 7.5 feet high and 12 feet long. The other two are the same height and 10 feet long. How many square feet of wallpaper would cover all four walls?
   Square feet for 12-foot wall = _____ x 2 = _____
   Square feet for 10-foot wall = _____ x 2 = _____

5. A clothes shop moved from a store that was 35 by 22 feet to a new location that was 53 by 32 feet. How many more square feet does the store have now?
   Square feet for first location = _____
   Square feet for new location = _____ Difference = _____

6. A school wanted to purchase a climber for the playground. The one they selected would need 98 square feet of space. The only space available on the playground was 12 feet long and 8 feet wide. Will there be enough space for the climber? _____

Area: Triangles

Finding the area of a triangle requires knowing the size of the base and the height. For the triangle formula, use **b** for **base** and **h** for **height**. Multiply $\frac{1}{2}$ times the size of the base and then multiply by the height. The answer will be in square units.

Example:

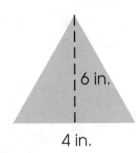

6 in.

4 in.

$$A = \frac{1}{2} \times b \times h$$

$$A = \frac{1}{2} \times 4 \times 6$$

$$A = 12 \text{ in.}^2$$

Directions: Apply the formula to find the area of each triangle below.

1.

3 in.   5 in.

4 in.

A = _____

2.

7 in.

5 in.

A = _____

3.

h = 6 in.

3 in.

A = _____

4.

2 in.

1 in.

A = _____

5. Diane wanted to make a sail for her new boat. The base of the triangular sail would be 7 feet and the height would be 6 feet. Find the area.

A = _____

Name: _____

Circles

The **circumference** is the distance around a circle. The **diameter** is the length of a line that divides the circle in half. The **radius** is the length of a line from the center of the circle to the outside edge. The formulas used to find the circumference and area of a circle include the Greek letter π (pronounced "pie"), which equals 3.14. To find the circumference (**C**) of a circle when you know the diameter (**d**), use this formula: $C = \pi \times d$. To find the circumference when you know the radius (**r**), use this formula: $C = \pi \times (r + r)$. To find the area (**A**) of a circle, use this formula: $A = \pi \times r \times r$.

Examples:

$C = \pi \times d$	$C = \pi \times (r + r)$	$A = \pi \times r \times r$
$C = 3.14 \times 15$	$C = 3.14 \times (3 + 3)$	$A = 3.14 \times 3 \times 3$
$C = 47.1$ inches	$C = 18.84$ inches	$A = 28.26$ in.^{2}

6 in.

15 in.

Directions: Solve the following problems. Round off the answers to the nearest hundredth where necessary.

1. Find the circumference of a circle with:

   a. A radius of 3.5 in.   C = _____   b. A diameter of 12 in.   C= _____

2. Find the area of both circles in #1:

   a. A = _____   b. A = _____

3. How many inches of tape would you need to go once around the middle of a ball that has a diameter of 7 inches? _____

4. Find the area of each figure below.

A.

B.
4 in.

A. A = _____

8 in.

4 in.

B. A = _____

C.

C. A = _____

8 in.

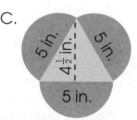
5 in. $4\frac{1}{2}$ in.   5 in.

5 in.

Name: _____

Volume

Volume is the number of cubic units that fills a space. A **cubic unit** has 6 equal sides, like a child's block. To find the volume (**V**) of something, multiply the length (**l**) by the width (**w**) by the height (**h**), or **V = l x w x h**. The answer will be in cubic units (^{3}). Sometimes it's easier to understand volume if you imagine a figure is made of small cubes.

Example: **V = l x w x h**
$V = 4 \times 6 \times 5$
$V = 120$ in.^{3}

Directions: Solve the following problems.

1. What is the volume of a cube that is 7 inches on each side? _____

2. How many cubic inches of cereal are in a box that is
    10 inches long, 6 inches wide and 4.5 inches high? _____

3. Jeremy made a tower of five blocks that are each 2.5 inches
    square. How many cubic inches are in his tower? _____

4. How many cubic feet of gravel are in the back of a full dump
    truck that measures 7 feet wide by 4 feet tall by 16 feet long? _____

5. Will 1,000 cubic inches of dirt fill a flower box that is 32 inches
    long, 7 inches wide and 7 inches tall? _____

6. A mouse needs 100 cubic inches of air to live for an hour.
    Will your pet mouse be okay for an hour in an airtight box
    that's 4.5 inches wide by 8.25 inches long by 2.5 inches high? _____

7. Find the volume of the figures below. 1 cube = 1 inch^3

A.
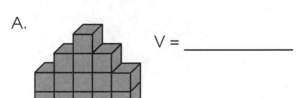
V = _____

C.
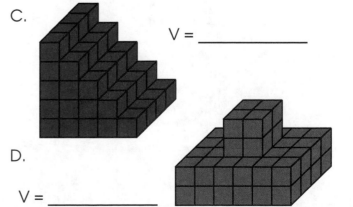
V = _____

B.
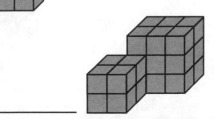
V = _____

D.
V = _____

59

Name: _____

Area Challenge

When finding the area of an unusual shape, first try to divide it into squares, rectangles or triangles. Find the area of each of those parts, then add your answers together to find the total area of the object.

Directions: Find the area of each shape below.

1.

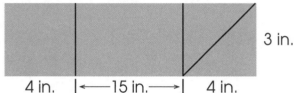

3 in.   3 in.

4 in. |←—15 in.—→| 4 in.

Total area = _____

2.

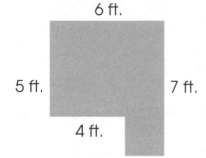

6 ft.

5 ft.   7 ft.

4 ft.

Total area = _____

3.

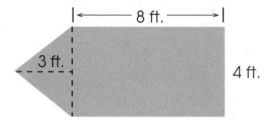

|←——— 8 ft. ———→|

3 ft.   4 ft.

Total area = _____

4.

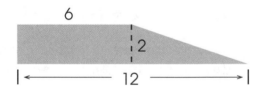

6

2

|←——— 12 ———→|

Total area = _____

5.

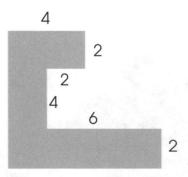

4

2

2

4

6

2

Total area = _____ units²

6.

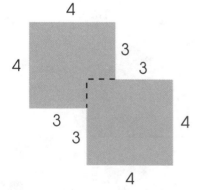

4

3

4   3

3   4

3

4

Total area = _____ units²

Lines

The following terms and definitions are used in geometry and represented by symbols.

Term	Definition	Symbol
Angle:	The amount of space where two lines meet	
Line:	A series of continuous points in a straight path, extending in either direction	
Line Segment:	A straight line extending from one exact point to another	
Intersecting Lines:	At least two straight lines that cross each other's paths	
Parallel Lines:	Lines that never get closer together or farther apart at any point	
Perpendicular Lines:	Two lines that intersect each other at a 90° angle	
Ray:	A straight line extending in one direction from one specific point	
Vertex:	The point at which two lines intersect	

Directions: Study the diagram and fill in the corresponding letters and symbols that represent the following:

1. a ray   _____

2. parallel lines   _____

3. a vertex   _____

4. line segment   _____

5. an angle   _____

6. perpendicular lines _____

7. intersecting lines _____

8. a line   _____

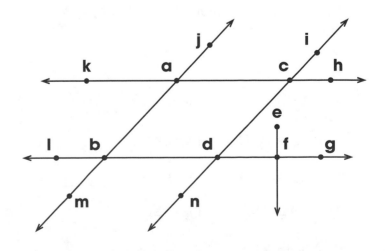

© 2001 McGraw-Hill.

Angles

Angles are named according to the number of degrees between the lines. The degrees are measured with a protractor.

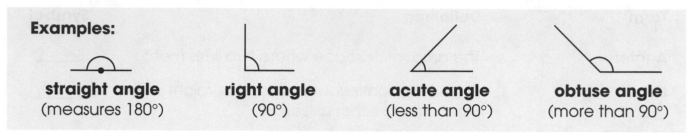

Examples:

straight angle
(measures 180°)

right angle
(90°)

acute angle
(less than 90°)

obtuse angle
(more than 90°)

Directions: Study the examples. Then follow the instructions below.

1. Use a protractor to measure each angle below. Then write whether it is straight, right, acute or obtuse.

A. Degrees: _____

Kind of angle: _____

C. Degrees: _____

Kind of angle: _____

B. _____ Degrees: _____

Kind of angle: _____

D. Degrees: _____

Kind of angle: _____

2. The angles in this figure are named by letters. Write the number of degrees in each angle and whether it is straight, right, acute or obtuse.

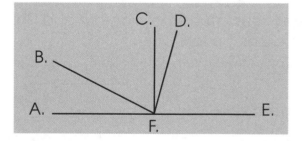

a. Angle AFB   Degrees: _____   Kind of angle: _____

b. Angle AFC   Degrees: _____   Kind of angle: _____

c. Angle AFD   Degrees: _____   Kind of angle: _____

d. Angle AFE   Degrees: _____   Kind of angle: _____

e. Angle BFD   Degrees: _____   Kind of angle: _____

Name: _____

Types of Triangles

The sum of angles in all triangles is 180°. However, triangles come in different shapes. They are categorized by the length of their sides and by their types of angles.

Equilateral:

Three equal sides

Isosceles:

Two equal sides

Scalene:

Zero equal sides

Acute:

Three acute angles

Right:

One right angle

Obtuse:

One obtuse angle

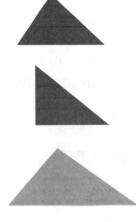

One triangle can be a combination of types, such as isosceles and obtuse.

Directions: Study the examples. Then complete the exercises below.

1. Read these directions and color in the correct triangles.

   Color the right scalene triangle blue.
   Color the obtuse scalene triangle red.
   Color the equilateral triangle yellow.
   Color the right isosceles triangle green.
   Color the acute isosceles triangle black.

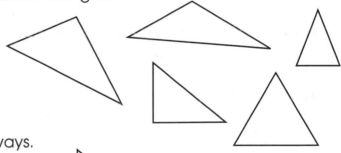

2. Describe each of these triangles in two ways.

   A. 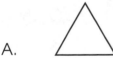   B.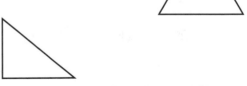

   _____ _____   _____ _____

3. In the space below, draw the following triangles.

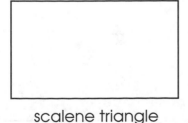
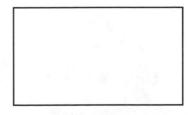

   scalene triangle   equilateral triangle   obtuse triangle

Name: _____

Finding Angles

All triangles have three angles. The sum of these angles is 180°. Therefore, if we know the number of degrees in two of the angles, we can add them together, then subtract from 180 to find the size of the third angle.

Directions: Follow the instructions below.

1. Circle the number that shows the third angle of triangles A through F. Then describe each triangle two ways. The first one has been done for you.

A. 60°, 60°	45° 50° (60°)	_equilateral, acute_
B. 35°, 55°	27° 90° 132°	_____
C. 30°, 120°	30° 74° 112°	_____
D. 15°, 78°	65° 87° 98°	_____
E. 28°, 93°	61° 59° 70°	_____
F. 12°, 114°	60° 50° 54°	_____

2. Find the number of degrees in the third angle of each triangle below.

A.

40°   40°

_____

B.

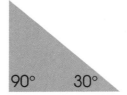

90°   30°

_____

C.

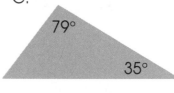

79°

35°

_____

D.

58°   62°

_____

E.

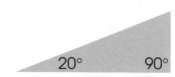

20°   90°

_____

F.

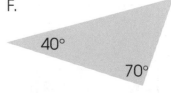

40°

70°

_____

Name:_____

Geometry Gems

Geometry is the study of lines and angles, the shapes they create and how they relate to one another.

Directions: Match the following shapes with their names.

A.

B.

C.

D.

E.

F.

acute _____   obtuse _____   isosceles _____

equilateral _____   scalene _____   right _____

Directions: Match the pictures with the correct terms.

A.

B.

C.

D.

E.

F.

line _____   line segment _____   ray _____

vertex _____   perpendicular lines _____   parallel Lines _____

Sam donated a piece of land that measures 220 feet by 100 yards. The city wants to build a soccer field on the land. They need at least 6,000 square yards to do this. Will the land Sam donated be large enough? _____

How much more land would the city need to purchase to build two soccer fields?

_____ (Find to the nearest whole number.)

Name: _____

Geometric Patterns

Geometric patterns can be described in several ways. **Similar shapes** have the same shape but in differing sizes. **Congruent shapes** have the same geometric pattern but may be facing in different directions. **Symmetrical shapes** are identical when divided in half.

Directions: Use the terms **similar**, **congruent** or **symmetrical** to describe the following patterns.

1.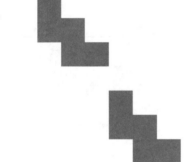

_____

2.

_____

3.

_____

4.

_____

5.

_____

6.

_____

7.

_____

Name:_____

Types of Quadrilaterals

A **quadrilateral** is a shape with four sides and four angles. The sum of angles in all quadrilaterals is 360°. Like triangles, quadrilaterals come in different shapes and are categorized by their sides and their angles.

A **square** has four parallel sides of equal length and four 90° angles.

A **rectangle** has four parallel sides, but only its opposite sides are equal length; it has four 90° angles.

A **parallelogram** has four parallel sides, with the opposite sides of equal length, but all its angles are more than or less than 90°.

A **trapezoid** has two opposite sides that are parallel; its sides may or may not be equal length; its angles may include none, one or two that are 90°.

Directions: Study the examples. Then complete the exercises below.

1. Color in the correct quadrilaterals.

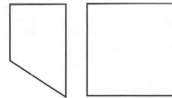
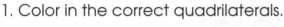
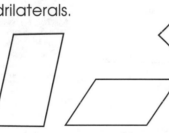
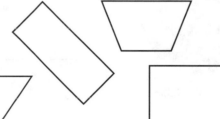

Color two squares blue.   Color two rectangles red.
Color two parallelograms yellow.   Color two trapezoids green.

2. Circle the number that shows the missing angle for each quadrilateral. Then name the possible quadrilaterals that could have those angles.

A. 90°, 90°, 90°	45°	90°	180°	_____
B. 65°, 115°, 65°	65°	90°	115°	_____
C. 90°, 110°, 90°	45°	70°	125°	_____
D. 100°, 80°, 80°	40°	80°	100°	_____
E. 90°, 120°, 50°	50°	75°	100°	_____

Review

Directions: Complete the following exercises.

1. Find the perimeter of this shape.

    P = _____

2. Find the area of each of these shapes.

    a.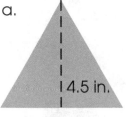

    A = _____

    b.

    A = _____

3. Find the circumference of these two circles.

    a.

    C = _____

    6 in. radius

    b.

    C = _____

    4.5 in. diameter

4. How many 1-in. sugar cubes could fit in a box 4 in. wide, 6 in. long and 3 in. high?

    V = _____

5. Describe each triangle below in two ways, using these terms: **equilateral**, **isosceles**, **scalene**, **acute**, **right**, **obtuse**.

    A.

    B.

    _____   _____

6. Circle the names of the quadrilaterals that can have 90° angles:

    square   rectangle   parallelogram   trapezoid

Name: _____

Length in Customary Units

The **customary system** of measurement is the most widely used in the United States.
It measures length in inches, feet, yards and miles.

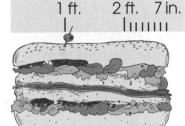

1 ft. 2 ft. 7 in.

Examples:

12 inches (in.) = 1 foot (ft.)
3 ft. (36 in.) = 1 yard (yd.)
5,280 ft. (1,760 yds.) = 1 mile (mi.)

To change to a larger unit, divide. To change to a smaller unit, multiply.

Examples:

To change inches to feet, divide by 12.	24 in. = 2 ft.	27 in. = 2 ft. 3 in.
To change feet to inches, multiply by 12.	3 ft. = 36 in.	4 ft = 48 in.
To change inches to yards, divide by 36.	108 in. = 3 yd.	80 in. = 2 yd. 8 in.
To change feet to yards, divide by 3.	12 ft. = 4 yd.	11 ft. = 3 yd. 2 ft.

Sometimes in subtraction you have to borrow units.

Examples:

$$
\begin{array}{ll}
3 \text{ ft. } 4 \text{ in.} & = 2 \text{ ft. } 16 \text{ in.} \\
- 1 \text{ ft. } 11 \text{ in.} & \underline{- 1 \text{ ft. } 11 \text{ in.}} \\
& 1 \text{ ft. } 5 \text{ in.}
\end{array}
$$

$$
\begin{array}{ll}
3 \text{ yd.} & = 2 \text{ yd. } 3 \text{ ft.} \\
- 1 \text{ yd. } 2 \text{ ft.} & \underline{- 1 \text{ yd. } 2 \text{ ft.}} \\
& 1 \text{ yd. } 1 \text{ ft.}
\end{array}
$$

Directions: Solve the following problems.

1. 108 in. = _____ ft.

2. 68 in. = _____ ft. _____ in.

3. 8 ft. = _____ yd. _____ ft.

4. 3,520 yd. = _____ mi.

5. What form of measurement (inches, feet, yards or miles) would you use for each
    item below?

    a. pencil _____

    b. vacation trip _____

    c. playground _____

    d. wall _____

6. One side of a square box is 2 ft. 4 in. What is the perimeter of the box? _____

7. Jason is 59 in. tall. Kent is 5 ft. 1 in. tall. Who is taller and by how much? _____

8. Karen bought a doll 2 ft. 8 in. tall for her little sister. She found a box
    that is 29 in. long. Will the doll fit in that box? _____

9. Dan's dog likes to go out in the backyard, which is 85 ft. wide. The dog's
    chain is 17 ft. 6 in. long. If Dan attaches one end of the chain to a pole
    in the middle of the yard, will his dog be able to leave the yard? _____

Name: _____

Length in Metric Units

The **metric system** measures length in meters, centimeters, millimeters, and kilometers.

Examples:
A **meter** (**m**) is about 40 inches or 3.3 feet.
A **centimeter** (**cm**) is $\frac{1}{100}$ of a meter or 0.4 inches.
A **millimeter** (**mm**) is $\frac{1}{1000}$ of a meter or 0.04 inches.
A **kilometer** (**km**) is 1,000 meters or 0.6 miles.

As before, divide to find a larger unit and multiply to find a smaller unit.

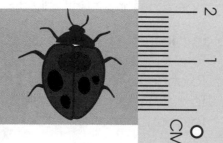

Examples:
To change cm to mm, multiply by 10.
To change cm to meters, divide by 100.
To change mm to meters, divide by 1,000.
To change km to meters, multiply by 1,000.

Directions: Solve the following problems.

1. 600 cm = _____ m   2. 12 cm = _____ mm   3. 47 m = _____ cm   4. 3 km = _____ m

5. In the sentences below, write the missing unit: m, cm, mm or km.

   a. A fingernail is about 1 _____ thick.

   b. An average car is about 5 _____ long.

   c. Someone could walk 1 _____ in 10 minutes.

   d. A finger is about 7 _____ long.

   e. A street could be 3 _____ long.

   f. The Earth is about 40,000 _____ around at the equator.

   g. A pencil is about 17 _____ long.

   h. A noodle is about 4 _____ wide.

   i. A teacher's desk is about 1 _____ wide.

6. A nickel is about 1 mm thick. How many nickels would be in a stack 1 cm high?   _____

7. Is something 25 cm long closer to 10 inches or 10 feet?   _____

8. Is something 18 mm wide closer to 0.7 inch or 7 inches?   _____

9. Would you get more exercise running 4 km or 500 m?   _____

10. Which is taller, something 40 m or 350 cm?   _____

Weight in Customary Units

Here are the main ways to measure weight in customary units:

16 ounces (oz.) = 1 pound (lb.)
2,000 lb. = 1 ton (tn.)
To change ounces to pounds, divide by 16.
To change pounds to ounces, multiply by 16.

As with measurements of length, you may have to borrow units in subtraction.

Example:

$$
\begin{array}{r}
4 \text{ lb. } 5 \text{ oz.} = 3 \text{ lb. } 21 \text{ oz.} \\
- 2 \text{ lb. } 10 \text{ oz.} \quad -2 \text{ lb. } 10 \text{ oz.} \\
\hline
1 \text{ lb. } 11 \text{ oz.}
\end{array}
$$

Directions: Solve the following problems.

1. 48 oz. = _____ lb.   2. 39 oz. = _____ lb.   3. 4 lb. = _____ oz.   4. 1.25 tn. = _____ lb.

5. What form of measurement would you use for each of these: ounces, pounds or tons?

 a. pencil _____   b. elephant _____   c. person _____

6. Which is heavier, 0.25 ton or 750 pounds?   _____

7. Twenty-two people, each weighing an average of 150 lb., want to get on an elevator that can carry up to 1.5 tons. Have many of them should wait for the next elevator?   _____

8. A truck is carrying 14 boxes that weigh 125 lb. each. It comes to a small bridge with a sign that says, "Bridge unsafe for trucks over 2 tons." Is it safe for the truck and the boxes to cross the bridge?   _____

9. A large box of Oat Boats contains 2 lb. 3 oz. of cereal, while a box of Honey Hunks contains 1 lb. 14 oz. How many more ounces are in the box of Oat Boats?   _____

10. A can of Peter's Powdered Drink Mix weighs 2 lb. 5 oz. A can of Petunia's Powdered Drink Mix weighs 40 oz. Which one is heavier?   _____

11. A can of Peter's Drink Mix is 12 cents an ounce. How much does it cost?   _____

12. How many 5-oz. servings could you get from a fish that weighs 3 lb. 12 oz.?   _____

Weight in Metric Units

A **gram** (**g**) is about 0.035 oz.
A **milligram** (**mg**) is $\frac{1}{1000}$ g or about 0.000035 oz.
A **kilogram** (**kg**) is 1,000 g or about 2.2 lb.
A **metric ton** (**t**) is 1,000 kg or about 1.1 tn.

To change g to mg, multiply by 1,000.
To change g to kg, divide by 1,000.
To change kg to g, multiply by 1,000.
To change t to kg, multiply by 1,000.

Directions: Solve the following problems.

1. 3 kg = _____ g

2. 2 g = _____ mg

3. 145 g = _____ kg

4. 3,000 kg = _____ t

5. _____ g = 450 mg

6. 3.5 t = _____ kg

7. Write the missing units below: g, mg, kg or t.

    a. A sunflower seed weighs less than 1 _____.

    b. A serving of cereal contains 14 _____ of sugar.

    c. The same serving of cereal has 250 _____ of salt.

    d. A bowling ball weighs about 7 _____.

    e. A whale weighs about 90 _____.

    f. A math textbook weighs about 1 _____.

    g. A safety pin weighs about 1 _____.

    h. An average car weighs about 1 _____.

8. Is 200 g closer to 7 oz. or 70 oz.? _____

9. Is 3 kg closer to 7 lb. or 70 lb.? _____

10. Does a metric ton weigh more or less than a ton measured by the customary system? _____

11. How is a kilogram different from a kilometer? _____

12. Which is heavier, 300 g or 1 kg? _____

Name: _____

Capacity in Customary Units

Here are the main ways to measure capacity (how much something will hold) in customary units:

8 fluid ounces (fl. oz.) = 1 cup (c.)
2 c. = 1 pint (pt.)
2 pt. = 1 quart (qt.)
4 qt. = 1 gallon (gal.)

To change ounces to cups, divide by 8.
To change cups to ounces, multiply by 8.
To change cups to pints or quarts, divide by 2.
To change pints to cups or quarts to pints, multiply by 2.

As with measurements of length and weight, you may have to borrow units in subtraction.

Example:	3 gal. 2 qt. =	2 gal. 6 qt.
	− 1 gal. 3 qt.	− 1 gal. 3 qt.
		1 gal. 3 qt.

Directions: Solve the following problems.

1. 32 fl. oz. = _____ pt.   2. 4 gal. = _____ pt.   3. _____ c. = 24 fl. oz.

4. 5 pt. = _____ qt.   5. 16 pt. = _____ gal.   6. 3 pt. = _____ fl. oz.

7. A large can of soup contains 19 fl. oz. A serving is about 8 oz. How many cans should you buy if you want to serve 7 people?   _____

8. A container of strawberry ice cream holds 36 fl. oz. A container of chocolate ice cream holds 2 pt. Which one has more ice cream? How much more?   _____

9. A day-care worker wants to give 15 children each 6 fl. oz. of milk. How many quarts of milk does she need?   _____

10. This morning, the day-care supervisor bought 3 gal. of milk. The kids drank 2 gal. 3 c. How much milk is left for tomorrow?   _____

11. Harriet bought 3 gal. 2 qt. of paint for her living room. She used 2 gal. 3 qt. How much paint is left over?   _____

12. Jason's favorite punch takes a pint of raspberry sherbet. If he wants to make $1\frac{1}{2}$ times the recipe, how many fl. oz. of sherbet does he need?   _____

Capacity in Metric Units

A **liter** (**L**) is a little over 1 quart.
A **milliliter** (**mL**) is $\frac{1}{1000}$ of a liter or about 0.03 oz.
A **kiloliter** (**kL**) is 1,000 liters or about 250 gallons.

Directions: Solve the following problems.

1. 5,000 mL = _____ L

2. 2,000 L = _____ kL

3. 3 L = _____ mL

4. Write the missing unit: L, mL or kL.

   a. A swimming pool holds about 100 _____ of water.

   b. An eyedropper is marked for 1 and 2 _____.

   c. A pitcher could hold 1 or 2 _____ of juice.

   d. A teaspoon holds about 5 _____ of medicine.

   e. A birdbath might hold 5 _____ of water.

   f. A tablespoon holds about 15 _____ of salt.

   g. A bowl holds about 250 _____ of soup.

   h. We drank about 4 _____ of punch at the party.

5. Which is more, 3 L or a gallon? _____

6. Which is more, 400 mL or 40 oz.? _____

7. Which is more, 1 kL or 500 L? _____

8. Is 4 L closer to a quart or a gallon? _____

9. Is 480 mL closer to 2 cups or 2 pints? _____

10. Is a mL closer to 4 drops or 4 teaspoonsful? _____

11. How many glasses of juice containing 250 mL
    each could you pour from a 1-L jug? _____

12. How much water would you need to water an
    average-sized lawn, 1 kL or 1 L? _____

Name:_____

Temperature in Customary and Metric Units

The customary system measures temperature in Fahrenheit (F°) degrees.

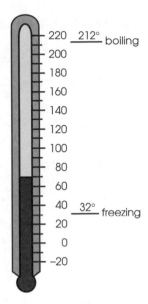

The metric system uses Celsius (C°) degrees.

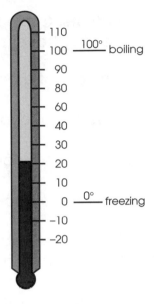

Directions: Study the thermometers and answer these questions.

1. Write in the temperature from both systems:

	Fahrenheit	**Celsius**
a. freezing	_____	_____
b. boiling	_____	_____
c. comfortable room temperature	_____	_____
d. normal body temperature	_____	_____

2. Underline the most appropriate temperature for both systems.

a. a reasonably hot day	34°	54°	84°	10°	20°	35°
b. a cup of hot chocolate	95°	120°	190°	60°	90°	120°
c. comfortable water to swim in	55°	75°	95°	10°	25°	40°

3. If the temperature is 35°C is it summer or winter? _____

4. Would ice cream stay frozen at 35°F? _____

5. Which is colder, –10°C or –10°F? _____

6. Which is warmer, 60°C or 60°F? _____

Customary and Metric Measures

Directions: Circle the units you would use to measure the following. Some may have more than one answer.

1. height of a basketball hoop   feet   inches   miles   kilometers

2. weight of a football player   ounces   pounds   kilograms   grams

3. length of a soccer field   miles   kilometers   feet   yards

4. circumference of a volleyball   inches   grams   centimeters   liters

5. distance a golf ball travels
    when hit by a club   kilometers   miles   yards   feet

6. weight of a referee's whistle   grams   ounces   pounds   kilograms

7. size of a tennis court   feet   inches   yards   kilometers

8. thickness of football
    shoulder pads   mm   km   oz.   in.

9. length of the bleachers at
    a stadium   kilograms   feet   meters   kilometers

10. capacity of the team's
    water cooler   liters   gallons   ounces   milliliters

11. temperature on game day   °Celsius   °Fahrenheit   grams   ounces

12. length of a golf club   millimeters   feet   inches   meters

13. speed a golf cart can travel   in. per hour mph   meters   grams

14. amount of water a player
    might drink during halftime
    of a game   ounces   liters   grams   pounds

15. the distance around a
    cross country course   mm   km   mi.   yd.

Name: _____

Comparing Measurements

Directions: Use the symbols >, < or = to make the following statements true.

1. 1 oz. ◯ 1 g

2. 10 kL ◯ 100 L

3. 25 cm ◯ 15 in.

4. 20 L ◯ 40 oz.

5. 60 oz. ◯ 2 lb.

6. 20 m ◯ 2 mi.

7. 2 gal. ◯ 2 L

8. 15 g ◯ 25 oz.

9. 35 ft. ◯ 12 yd.

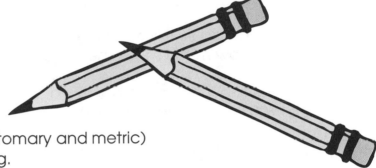

Directions: Write which units (both customary and metric) you would use to measure the following.

	Metric	Customary
1. volume	_____	_____
2. mass of a car	_____	_____
3. temperature	_____	_____
4. distance between cities	_____	_____
5. length of a pencil	_____	_____
6. weight of a box of cereal	_____	_____
7. glass of milk	_____	_____
8. height of a friend	_____	_____

Name: _____

Review

Directions: Complete the following exercises.

1. 372 in. = _____ yd. _____ ft.

2. 4 km = _____ m

3. 1.25 lb. = _____ oz.

4. 2,000 mg = _____ g

5. 1 qt. = _____ oz.

6. 10,000 mL = _____ L

7. Todd has a board that is 6 ft. 3 in. long. He needs to cut it to 4 ft. 9 in. How much should he cut off?

   _____

8. In a contest, Joyce threw a ball 12 yd. 2 ft. Brenda threw the ball 500 in. Who threw the farthest?

   _____

9. Would you measure this workbook in mm or cm?

   _____

10. Which is heavier, a box of books that weigh 4 lb. 6 oz. or a box of dishes that weigh 80 oz.?

    _____

11. A 1-lb. package has 10 hot dogs. How much of an ounce does each hot dog weigh?

    _____

12. Would the amount of salt (sodium) in 1 oz. of potato chips be 170 g or 170 mg?

    _____

13. If someone ate half of a gallon of ice cream, how many fluid ounces would be left?

    _____

14. You want to serve 6 fl. oz. of ice cream to each of 16 friends at your party. How many quarts of ice cream should you buy?

    _____

15. Would you measure water in a fish pond with L or kL?

    _____

16. Would popsicles melt at 5°C?

    _____

17. Would soup be steaming hot at 100°F?

    _____

Name: _____

Ratios

A **ratio** is a comparison of two quantities. For example, a wall is 96 in. high; a pencil is 8 in. long. By dividing 8 into 96, you find it would take 12 pencils to equal the height of the wall. The ratio, or comparison, of the wall to the pencil can be written three ways: 1 to 12; 1:12; $\frac{1}{12}$. In this example, the ratio of triangles to circles is 4:6. The ratio of triangles to squares is 4:9. The ratio of circles to squares is 6:9. These ratios will stay the same if we divide both numbers in the ratio by the same number.

Examples: $\frac{4 \div 2 = 2}{6 \div 2 = 3}$ $\frac{6 \div 3 = 2}{9 \div 3 = 3}$ (There is no number that will divide into both 4 and 9.)

By reducing 4:6 and 6:9 to their lowest terms, they are the same—2:3. This means that 2:3, 4:6 and 6:9 are all equal ratios. You can also find equal ratios for all three by multiplying both numbers of the ratio by the same number.

Examples: $\frac{4 \times 3 = 12}{6 \times 3 = 18}$ $\frac{6 \times 5 = 30}{9 \times 5 = 45}$ $\frac{4 \times 4 = 16}{9 \times 4 = 36}$

Directions: Solve the following problems.

1. Write two more equal ratios for each of the following by multiplying or dividing both numbers in the ratio by the same number.

   a. $\frac{1}{2}$ $\frac{2}{4}$ $\frac{3}{6}$ _____ _____   b. $\frac{1}{4}$ $\frac{2}{8}$ $\frac{4}{16}$ _____ _____   c. $\frac{8}{24}$ $\frac{1}{3}$ $\frac{3}{9}$ _____ _____

2. Circle the ratios that are equal.

   a. $\frac{1}{6}$ $\frac{3}{6}$ b. $\frac{15}{25}$ $\frac{3}{5}$ c. $\frac{2}{7}$ $\frac{10}{35}$ d. $\frac{2}{3}$ $\frac{6}{10}$

3. Write each ratio three ways.

   a. stars to crosses _____

   b. crosses to trees _____

   c. stars to all other shapes _____

4. Write two equal ratios (multiplying or dividing) for:

   a. stars to crosses _____

   b. crosses to trees _____

   c. stars to all other shapes _____

Missing Numbers in Ratios

You can find a missing number (*n*) in an equal ratio. First, figure out which number has already been multiplied to get the number you know. (In the first example, 3 is multiplied by 3 to get 9; in the second example, 2 is multiplied by 6 to get 12.) Then multiply the other number in the ratio by the same number (3 and 6 in the examples).

Examples: $\frac{3}{4} = \frac{9}{n}$ $\frac{3}{4} \times \frac{3}{3} = \frac{9}{12}$ $n = 12$ $\frac{1}{2} = \frac{n}{12}$ $\frac{1}{2} \times \frac{6}{6} = \frac{6}{12}$ $n = 6$

Directions: Solve the following problems.

1. Find each missing number.

a. $\frac{1}{2} = \frac{n}{12}$ $n =$ _____

b. $\frac{1}{5} = \frac{n}{15}$ $n =$ _____

c. $\frac{3}{2} = \frac{18}{n}$ $n =$ _____

d. $\frac{5}{8} = \frac{n}{32}$ $n =$ _____

e. $\frac{8}{3} = \frac{16}{n}$ $n =$ _____

f. $\frac{n}{14} = \frac{5}{7}$ $n =$ _____

2. If a basketball player makes 9 baskets in 12 tries, what is her ratio of baskets to tries, in lowest terms?

_____

3. At the next game, the player has the same ratio of baskets to tries. If she tries 20 times, how many baskets should she make?

_____

4. At the third game, she still has the same ratio of baskets to tries. This time she makes 12 baskets. How many times did she probably try?

_____

5. If a driver travels 40 miles in an hour, what is his ratio of miles to minutes, in lowest terms?

_____

6. At the same speed, how far would the driver travel in 30 minutes?

_____

7. At the same speed, how long would it take him to travel 60 miles?

_____

Ratio Review

Directions: Use the bird-watching data from the chart to complete the following exercises.

Species	Day 1	Day 2	Day 3
Robin	12	20	10
Cardinal	9	12	9
Sparrow	22	24	26
Blue Jay	7	7	14
Woodpecker	3	6	9
Purple FInch	5	10	5
House Wren	18	9	12

1. Find the ratio between the following sets of birds for all days.

   blue jay to cardinal   _____ to _____

   robin to sparrow   _____ to _____

   purple finch to house wren   _____ to _____

   woodpecker to blue jay   _____ to _____

2. State the ratio of each for the first and second day, and the second and third day.

   cardinal   _____ to _____ and _____ to _____

   robin   _____ to _____ and _____ to _____

   sparrow   _____ to _____ and _____ to _____

   blue jay   _____ to _____ and _____ to _____

   woodpecker   _____ to _____ and _____ to _____

   purple finch _____ to _____ and _____ to _____

   house wren   _____ to _____ and _____ to _____

3. Which birds have equivalent ratios? _____

4. What process did you use to find the equal ratios? _____

5. How could you tell if two ratios are not equivalent? _____

_____

Proportions

A **proportion** is a statement that two ratios are equal. To make sure ratios are equal, called a proportion, we multiply the cross products.

Examples of proportions: $\frac{1}{5} = \frac{2}{10}$ $\frac{1}{2} \times \frac{10}{5} = \frac{10}{10}$ $\frac{3}{7} = \frac{15}{35}$ $\frac{3}{7} \times \frac{35}{15} = \frac{105}{105}$

These two ratios are not a proportion: $\frac{4}{3} = \frac{5}{6}$ $\frac{4}{3} \times \frac{6}{5} = \frac{24}{15}$

To find a missing number (n) in a proportion, multiply the cross products and divide.

Examples: $\frac{n}{30} = \frac{1}{6}$ $n \times 6 = 1 \times 30$ $n \times 6 = 30$
$$n = \frac{30}{6}$$
$$n = 5$$

Directions: Solve the following problems.

1. Write = between the ratios if they are a proportion. Write ≠ if they are not a proportion. The first one has been done for you.

   a. $\frac{1}{2}$ ⬭= $\frac{6}{12}$ b. $\frac{13}{18}$ ◯ $\frac{20}{22}$ c. $\frac{2}{6}$ ◯ $\frac{5}{15}$ d. $\frac{5}{6}$ ◯ $\frac{20}{24}$

2. Find the missing numbers in these proportions.

   a. $\frac{2}{5} = \frac{n}{15}$ $n =$ _____   b. $\frac{3}{8} = \frac{9}{n}$ $n =$ _____   c. $\frac{n}{18} = \frac{4}{12}$ $n =$ _____

3. One issue of a magazine costs $2.99, but if you buy a subscription, 12 issues cost $35.99. Is the price at the same proportion?   _____

4. A cookie recipe calls for 3 cups of flour to make 36 cookies. How much flour is needed for 48 cookies?   _____

5. The same recipe requires 4 teaspoons of cinnamon for 36 cookies. How many teaspoons is needed to make 48 cookies? (Answer will include a fraction.)   _____

6. The recipe also calls for 2 cups of sugar for 36 cookies. How much sugar should you use for 48 cookies? (Answer will include a fraction.)   _____

7. If 2 kids can eat 12 cookies, how many can 8 kids eat?   _____

Percents

Percent means "per 100." A percent is a ratio that compares a number with 100. The same number can be written as a decimal and a percent. To change a decimal to a percent, move the decimal point two places to the right and add the % sign. To change a percent to a decimal, drop the % sign and place a decimal point two places to the left.

Examples: 0.25 = 25%   0.1 = 10%   1.456 = 145.6%
          32% = 0.32   99% = 0.99   203% = 2.03

A percent or decimal can also be written as a ratio or fraction.

Example: $0.25 = 25\% = \frac{25}{100} = \frac{1}{4} = 1:4$

To change a fraction or ratio to a percent, first change it to a decimal. Divide the numerator by the denominator.

Examples: $\frac{1}{3} = 3\overline{)1.00}$ $0.33\frac{1}{3} = 33\frac{1}{3}\%$ $\frac{2}{5} = 5\overline{)2.0}$ $0.4 = 40\%$

Directions: Solve the following problems.

1. Change the percents to decimals.

   a. 3% = _____   b. 75% = _____   c. 14% = _____   d. 115% = _____

2. Change the decimals and fractions to percents.

   a. 0.56 = _____ %   b. 0.03 = _____ %   c. $\frac{3}{4}$ = _____ %   d. $\frac{1}{5}$ = _____ %

3. Change the percents to ratios in their lowest terms. The first one has been done for you.

   a. 75% = $\underline{\frac{75}{100} = \frac{3}{4} = \textbf{3:4}}$ b. 40% = _____

   c. 35% = _____   d. 70% = _____

4. The class was 45% girls. What percent was boys?   _____

5. Half the shoes in one store were on sale. What percent
   of the shoes were their ordinary price?   _____

6. Kim read 84 pages of a 100-page book. What percent
   of the book did she read?   _____

Percents

To find the percent of a number, change the percent to a decimal and multiply.

Examples: 45% of $20 = 0.45 x $20 = $9.00
125% of 30 = 1.25 x 30 = 37.50

Directions: Solve the following problems. Round off the answers to the nearest hundredth where necessary.

1. Find the percent of each number.

   a. 26% of 40 = _____   b. 12% of 329 = _____

   c. 73% of 19 = _____   d. 2% of 24 = _____

2. One family spends 35% of its weekly budget of $150 on food. How much do they spend?   _____

3. A shirt in a store usually costs $15.99, but today it's on sale for 25% off. The clerk says you will save $4.50. Is that true?   _____

4. A book that usually costs $12 is on sale for 25% off. How much will it cost?   _____

5. After you answer 60% of 150 math problems, how many do you have left to do?   _____

6. A pet store's shipment of tropical fish was delayed. Nearly 40% of the 1,350 fish died. About how many lived?   _____

7. The shipment had 230 angelfish, which died in the same proportion as the other kinds of fish. About how many angelfish died?   _____

8. A church youth group was collecting cans of food. Their goal was 1,200 cans, but they exceeded their goal by 25%. How many cans did they collect?   _____

Name:_____

Percents

When working with percents, think of them as fractions with a denominator of 100. To calculate the percent of any number, first change the percent to a decimal and then multiply the two numbers.

Example: $15\% = \dfrac{15}{100}$ 15% of 25 = 0.15 x 25 = 3.75

Directions: Solve the following problems.

1. Brian collected 93 buckeyes from a tree in his grandmother's yard. He wanted to share some of them with his friends at school. If he gave away 40, what percent did he keep for himself?   _____

2. As part of a science project, Brian planted 10 buckeyes on Saturday and 6 more on the following Tuesday. Two weeks later, 4 tiny sprouts emerged from the soil. When Brian wrote his science report, he listed his project as having a success rate of what percent?   _____

3. While sorting the buckeyes, Brian found that only 7% of them had a diameter larger than 1.5 inches, 31% had a diameter of about 1 inch and the remaining 62% were less than 1 inch. How many buckeyes were in each group?

    _____

    _____

    _____

4. Brian used 30 buckeyes to make keychains for a craft show. It took him $\frac{1}{4}$ of an hour to make each one. He finished 9 of them the first day. What percent of the project did he have done and how much time will he need to complete the whole project?   _____%

    time:_____

5. Brian wanted to earn money to buy a science book about buckeye trees. He sold the keychains for $3 each at the craft show and collected $60. What percent of his product did he have left?

    _____

6. Calculate the percentages.

    60% of 99 = _____   30% of 49 = _____   75% of 12 = _____

    29% of 100 = _____   20% of 250 = _____   17% of 175 = _____

Probability

Probability is the ratio of favorable outcomes to possible outcomes in an experiment. You can use probability (P) to figure out how likely something is to happen. For example, six picture cards are turned facedown—3 cards have stars, 2 have triangles and 1 has a circle. What is the probability of picking the circle? Using the formula below, you have a 1 in 6 probability of picking the circle, a 2 in 6 probability of picking a triangle and a 3 in 6 probability of picking a star.

Example: $\underline{P = \text{number of favorable outcomes}}$ $P = \dfrac{1}{6} = 1{:}6$
number of trials

Directions: Solve the following problems.

1. A class has 14 girls and 15 boys. If all of their names are put on separate slips in a hat, what is the probability of each person's name being chosen? _____

2. In the same class, what is the probability that a girl's name will be chosen? _____

3. In this class, 3 boys are named Mike. What is the probability that a slip with "Mike" written on it will be chosen? _____

4. A spinner on a board game has the numbers 1–8. What is the probability of spinning and getting a 4? _____

5. A paper bag holds these colors of wooden beads: 4 blue, 5 red and 6 yellow. If you select a bead without looking, do you have an equal probability of getting each color? _____

6. Using the same bag of beads, what is the probability of reaching in and drawing out a red bead (in lowest terms)? _____

7. In the same bag, what is the probability of not getting a blue bead? _____

8. In a carnival game, plastic ducks have spots. The probability of picking a duck with a yellow spot is 2:15. There is twice as much probability of picking a duck with a red spot. What is the probability of picking a duck with a red spot? _____

9. In this game, all the other ducks have green spots. What is the probability of picking a duck with a green spot (in lowest terms)? _____

Name: _____

Possible Combinations

Today the cafeteria is offering 4 kinds of sandwiches, 3 kinds of drinks and 2 kinds of cookies. How many possible combinations could you make? To find out, multiply the number of choices together.

Example: 4 x 3 x 2 = 24 possible combinations

Directions: Solve the following problems.

1. If Juan has 3 shirts and 4 pairs of shorts, how many combinations can he make? _____

2. Janice can borrow 1 book and 1 magazine at a time from her classroom library. The library has 45 books and 16 magazines. How many combinations are possible? _____

3. Kerry's mother is redecorating the living room. She has narrowed her choices to 6 kinds of wallpaper, 3 shades of paint and 4 colors of carpeting that all match. How many possible combinations are there? _____

4. Pam has 6 sweaters that she can combine with pants to make 24 outfits. How many pairs of pants does she have? _____

5. Kenny can get to school by walking, taking a bus, riding his bike or asking his parents for a ride. He can get home the same ways, except his parents aren't available then. How many combinations can he make of ways to get to school and get home? _____

6. Sue's middle school offers 3 different language classes, 3 art classes and 2 music classes. If she takes one class in each area, how many possible combinations are there? _____

7. Bart's school offers 4 language classes, 3 art classes and some music classes. If Bart can make 36 possible combinations, how many music classes are there? _____

8. AAA Airlines schedules 12 flights a day from Chicago to Atlanta. Four of those flights go on to Orlando. From the Orlando airport you can take a bus, ride in a taxi or rent a car to get to Disneyworld. How many different ways are there to get from Chicago to Disneyworld if you make part of your trip on AAA Airlines? _____

Name: _____

Review

Directions: Solve the following problems. Round answers to the nearest hundredth where necessary.

1. Write an equal ratio for each of these:

   a. $\dfrac{1}{7}$ = _____

   b. $\dfrac{5}{8}$ = _____

   c. $\dfrac{15}{3}$ = _____

   d. $\dfrac{6}{24}$ = _____

2. State the ratios below in lowest terms.

   a. cats to bugs = _____

   b. cats to dogs = _____

   c. dogs to all other objects = _____

3. If Shawn drives 45 miles an hour, how far could he go in 40 minutes? _____

4. At the same speed, how many minutes would it take Shawn to drive 120 miles? _____

5. Mr. Herman is building a doghouse in proportion to his family's house. The family's house is 30 ft. high and the doghouse is 5 ft. high. If the family house is 42 ft. wide, how wide should the doghouse be? _____

6. The family house is 24 ft. from front to back. How big should Mr. Herman make the doghouse? _____

7. Change these numbers to percents:

   a. 0.56 = _____

   b. $\dfrac{4}{5}$ = _____

   c. 0.04 = _____

   d. $\dfrac{3}{8}$ = _____

8. Which is a better deal, a blue bike for $125 at 25% off or a red bike for $130 at 30% off? _____

9. If sales tax is 6%, what would be the total price of the blue bike? _____

10. Richard bought 6 raffle tickets for a free bike. If 462 tickets were sold, what is Richard's probability of winning? _____

11. Lori bought 48 tickets in the same raffle. What are her chances of winning? _____

Name: _____

Review

Directions: Follow the instructions below. Write >, < or =.

1. $\dfrac{20}{25}$ ◯ $\dfrac{3}{5}$ 2. $\dfrac{1}{7}$ ◯ $\dfrac{7}{28}$ 3. $\dfrac{1}{3}$ ◯ $\dfrac{8}{24}$

Find the missing numbers.

1. $\dfrac{1}{3} = \dfrac{n}{15}$ $n =$ _____

2. $\dfrac{4}{5} = \dfrac{16}{n}$ $n =$ _____

3. $\dfrac{n}{14} = \dfrac{1}{7}$ $n =$ _____

Find the answers.

1. 30% of 25 = _____   2. 64% of 100 = _____

3. 16% of 47 = _____   4. 75% of 60 = _____

Change the percents to ratios.

1. 50% _____   2. 80% _____

3. 20% _____   4. 35% _____

While getting dressed for school early one morning, the light in Toni's bedroom burned out. Toni knew he had plenty of clean socks in his drawer, but none of them were matched. He had 24 white socks and 6 blue socks. What is the probability of Toni finding 2 white socks or 2 blue socks in the dark?

white _____   blue _____

Name: _____

Comparing Data

Data (**datum**—singular) are gathered information. The **range** is the difference between the highest and lowest number in a group of numbers. The **median** is the number in the middle when numbers are listed in order. The **mean** is the average of the numbers. We can compare numbers or data by finding the range, median and mean.

Example: 16, 43, 34, 78, 8, 91, 26

To compare these numbers, we first need to put them in order: 8 16 26 34 43 78 91. By subtracting the lowest number (8) from the highest one (91), we find the range: 83. By finding the number that falls in the middle, we have the median: 34 (If no number fell exactly in the middle, we would average the two middle numbers.) By adding them and dividing by the number of numbers (7), we get the mean: 42.29 (rounded to the nearest hundredth).

Directions: Solve the following problems. Round answers to the nearest hundredth where necessary.

1. Find the range, median and mean of these numbers: 19, 5, 84, 27, 106, 38, 75.

   Range: _____   Median: _____   Mean: _____

2. Find the range, median and mean finishing times for 6 runners in a race. Here are their times in seconds: 14.2, 12.9, 13.5, 10.3, 14.8, 14.7.

   Range: _____   Median: _____   Mean: _____

3. If the runner who won the race in 10.3 seconds had run even faster and finished in 7 seconds, would the mean time be higher or lower?   _____

4. If that runner had finished in 7 seconds, what would be the median time?   _____

5. Here are the high temperatures in one city for a week: 65, 72, 68, 74, 81, 68, 85. Find the range, median and mean temperatures.

   Range: _____   Median: _____   Mean: _____

6. Find the range, median and mean test scores for this group of students: 41, 32, 45, 36, 48, 38, 37, 42, 39, 36.

   Range: _____   Median: _____   Mean: _____

Tables

Organizing data into tables makes it easier to compare numbers. As evident in the example, putting many numbers in a paragraph is confusing. When the same numbers are organized in a table, you can compare numbers in a glance. Tables can be arranged several ways and still be easy to read and understand.

Example: Money spent on groceries:
Family A: week 1 — $68.50; week 2 — $72.25; week 3 — $67.00; week 4 — $74.50.
Family B: week 1 — $42.25; week 2 — $47.50; week 3 — $50.25; week 4 — $53.50.

	Week 1	**Week 2**	**Week 3**	**Week 4**
Family A	$68.50	$72.25	$67.00	$74.50
Family B	$45.25	$47.50	$50.25	$53.50

Directions: Complete the following exercises.

1. Finish the table below, then answer the questions.
   Data: Steve weighs 230 lb. and is 6 ft. 2 in. tall. George weighs 218 lb. and is 6 ft. 3 in. tall. Chuck weighs 225 lb. and is 6 ft. 1 in. tall. Henry weighs 205 lb. and is 6 ft. tall.

	Henry	**George**	**Chuck**	**Steve**
Weight				
Height				

   a. Who is tallest?_____ b. Who weighs the least?_____

2. On another sheet of paper, prepare 2 tables comparing the amount of money made by 3 booths at the school carnival this year and last year. In the first table, write the names of the games in the left-hand column (like **Family A** and **Family B** in the example). In the second table (using the same data), write the years in the left-hand column. Here is the data: fish pond—this year $15.60, last year $13.50; bean-bag toss—this year $13.45, last year $10.25; ring toss—this year $23.80, last year $18.80. After you complete both tables, answer the following questions.

   a. Which booth made the most money this year? _____

   b. Which booth made the biggest improvement from last year to this year? _____

Name: _____

Bar Graphs

Another way to organize information is a **bar graph**. The bar graph in the example compares the number of students in 4 elementary schools. Each bar stands for 1 school. You can easily see that School A has the most students and School C has the least. The numbers along the left show how many students attend each school.

Example:

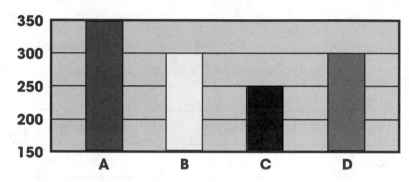

Directions: Complete the following exercises.

1. This bar graph will show how many calories are in 1 serving of 4 kinds of cereal. Draw the bars the correct height and label each with the name of the cereal. After completing the bar graph, answer the questions. Data: Korn Kernals—150 calories; Oat Floats—160 calories; Rite Rice—110 calories; Sugar Shapes—200 calories.

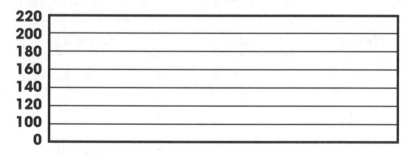

A. Which cereal is the best to eat if you're trying to lose weight? _____

B. Which cereal has nearly the same number of calories as Oat Floats? _____

2. On another sheet of paper, draw your own graph, showing the number of TV commercials in 1 week for each of the 4 cereals in the graph above. After completing the graph, answer the questions. Data: Oat Boats—27 commercials; Rite Rice—15; Sugar Shapes—35; Korn Kernals—28.

A. Which cereal is most heavily advertised? _____

B. What similarities do you notice between the graph of calories and the graph of TV commercials? _____

Name:_____

Picture Graphs

Newspapers and textbooks often use pictures in graphs instead of bars. Each picture stands for a certain number of objects. Half a picture means half the number. The picture graph in the example indicates the number of games each team won. The Astros won 7 games, so they have $3\frac{1}{2}$ balls.

Example:

	Games Won			
Astros	⚾	⚾	⚾	◖
Orioles	⚾	⚾		
Bluebirds	⚾	⚾	⚾	⚾
Sluggers	⚾			

(1 ball = 2 games)

Directions: Complete the following exercises.

Finish this picture graph, showing the number of students who have dogs in 4 sixth-grade classes. Draw simple dogs in the graph, letting each drawing stand for 2 dogs.
Data: Class 1—12 dogs; Class 2—16 dogs; Class 3—22 dogs; Class 4—12 dogs.
After completing the graph, answer the questions.

	Dogs Owned by Students
Class 1	
Class 2	
Class 3	
Class 4	

(One dog drawing = 2 students' dogs)

1. Why do you think newspapers use picture graphs?_____

_____

2. Would picture graphs be appropriate to show exact number of dogs living in America? Why or why not?_____

_____

Line Graphs

Still another way to display information is a line graph. The same data can often be shown in both a bar graph and a line graph. Nevertheless, line graphs are especially useful in showing changes over a period of time.

The line graph in the example shows changes in the number of students enrolled in a school over a 5-year period. Enrollment was highest in 1988 and has decreased gradually each year since then. Notice how labeling the years and enrollment numbers make the graph easy to understand.

Example:

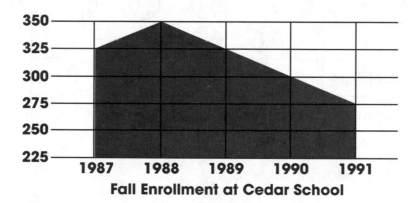

Fall Enrollment at Cedar School

Directions: Complete the following exercises.

1. On another sheet of paper, draw a line graph that displays the growth of a corn plant over a 6-week period. Mark the correct points, using the data below, and connect them with a line. After completing the graph, answer the questions. Data: week 1—3.5 in.; week 2—4.5 in.; week 3—5 in.; week 4—5.5 in.; week 5—5.75 in.; week 6—6 in.

   a. Between which weeks was the growth fastest?   _____

   b. Between which weeks was the growth slowest?   _____

2. On another sheet of paper draw a line graph to show how the high temperature varied during one week. Then answer the questions. Data: Sunday—high of 53 degrees; Monday—51; Tuesday—56; Wednesday—60; Thursday—58; Friday—67; Saturday—73. Don't forget to label the numbers.

   a. In general, did the days get warmer or cooler?   _____

   b. Do you think this data would have been as clear in a bar graph? _____
      Explain your answer.

   _____

   _____

Circle Graphs

Circle graphs are useful in showing how something is divided into parts. The circle graph in the example shows how Carly spent her $10 allowance. Each section is a fraction of her whole allowance. For example, the movie tickets section is $\frac{1}{2}$ of the circle, showing that she spent $\frac{1}{2}$ of her allowance, $5, on movie tickets.

Directions: Complete the following exercises.

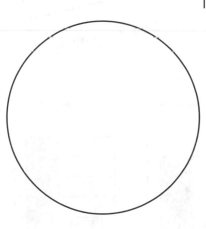

1. When the middle school opened last fall, $\frac{1}{2}$ of the students came from East Elementary, $\frac{1}{4}$ came from West Elementary, $\frac{1}{8}$ came from North Elementary and the remaining students moved into the town from other cities. Make a circle graph showing these proportions. Label each section. Then answer the questions.

   a. What fraction of students at the new school moved into the area from other cities? _____

   b. If the new middle school has 450 students enrolled, how many used to go to East Elementary? _____

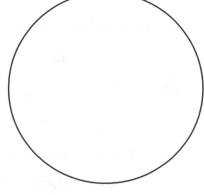

2. This circle graph will show the hair color of 24 students in one class. Divide the circle into 4 sections to show this data: black hair—8 students; brown hair—10 students; blonde hair—4 students; red hair—2 students. (Hint: 8 students are $\frac{8}{24}$ or $\frac{1}{3}$ of the class.) Be sure to label each section by hair color. Then answer the questions.

   a. Looking at your graph, what fraction of the class is the combined group of blonde- and red-haired students? _____

   b. Which two fractions of hair color combine to total half the class? _____

MATH 6

Comparing Presentation Methods

Tables and different kinds of graphs have different purposes. Some are more helpful for certain kinds of information. The table and three graphs below all show basically the same information—the amount of money Mike and Margaret made in their lawn-mowing business over a 4-month period.

Combined Income per Month

	Mike	Margaret
June	$34	$36
July	41	35
August	27	28
Sept.	36	40
Totals	$138	$139

Combined Income per Month

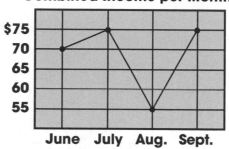

June   July   Aug.   Sept.

Combined Income per Month

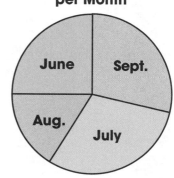

Combined Income per Month

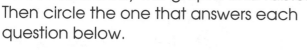

June   July   Aug.   Sept.

Directions: Study the graphs and table. Then circle the one that answers each question below.

1. Which one shows the fraction of the total income that Mike and Margaret made in August?

     table   line graph   bar graph   circle graph

2. Which one compares Mike's earnings with Margaret's?

     table   line graph   bar graph   circle graph

3. Which one has the most exact numbers?

     table   line graph   bar graph   circle graph

4. Which one has no numbers?

     table   line graph   bar graph   circle graph

5. Which two best show how Mike and Margaret's income changed from month to month?

     table   line graph   bar graph   circle graph

Graphing Data

Directions: Complete the following exercises.

1. Use the following information to create a bar graph.

Cities	Population (in 1,000's)
Dover	20
Newton Falls	12
Springdale	25
Hampton	17
Riverside	5

2. Study the data and create a line graph showing the number of baskets Jonah scored during the season.

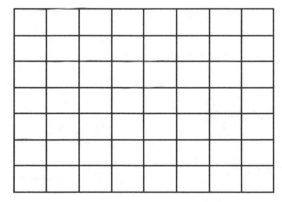

Game 1 — 10

Game 2 — 7

Game 3 — 11

Game 4 — 10

Game 5 — 9

Game 6 — 5

Game 7 — 9

Fill in the blanks.

a. High game: _____

b. Low game: _____

c. Average baskets per game: _____

3. Study the graph, then answer the questions.

a. Which flavor is the most popular? _____

b. Which flavor sold the least? _____

c. What decimal represents the two highest sellers? _____

d. Which flavor had $\frac{1}{10}$ of the sales? _____

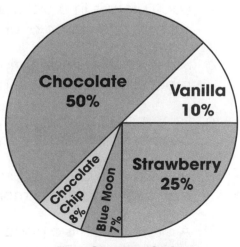

Ice-Cream Sales

Name: _____

Review

Directions: Complete the following exercises.

1. Joseph's older sister and 3 of her friends work
   at fast-food restaurants. Here is what they each
   make an hour: $3.85, $4.20, $3.95, $4.65.
   Find the range, median and mean of their earnings.

   range: _____   median: _____   mean: _____

2. If the person who makes $3.85 gets a 5-cent raise, what will
   be the median?   _____

3. Write **T** for true or **F** for false:

   a. If you include dates in a table, you must write them across the
      top or bottom of the table, not in the left-hand column.   _____

   b. Tables allow you to show small differences between numbers. _____

   c. A bar graph allows you to compare the amount of alcohol
      in different kinds of liquor.   _____

   d. A bar graph allows you to show small differences
      between numbers.   _____

   e. Picture graphs are used only in children's books.   _____

   f. Each picture in a picture graph equals one unit of something,
      such as one gallon of oil or one person.   _____

   g. Some kinds of information can be shown equally well in both
      a bar graph and a line graph.   _____

   h. Labeling types of information on a graph is not necessary
      because the reader can figure it out.   _____

   i. A line graph allows you to show changes in the popularity of
      a TV show month by month.   _____

   j. A circle graph is a good way to show changes in the
      popularity of a TV show over time.   _____

Name: _____

Integers

An **integer** is a whole number above or below 0: –2, –1, 0, +1, +2, and so on. **Opposite integers** are two integers the same distance from 0, but in different directions, such as –2 and +2.

Think of the water level in the picture as 0. The part of the iceberg sticking out of the water is positive. The iceberg has +3 feet above water. The part of the iceberg below the water is negative. The iceberg extends – 9 feet under water.

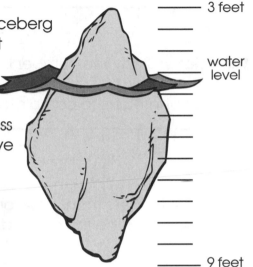

——— 3 feet
————
————
water level
————
————
————
————
——— 9 feet

Numbers greater than 0 are **positive** numbers. Numbers less than 0 are **negative** numbers. Pairs of positive and negative numbers are called **opposite integers**.

Examples of opposite integers:
–5 and +5
losing 3 pounds and gaining 3 pounds
earning $12 and spending $12

Directions: Complete the following exercises.

1. Write each of these as an integer. The first one is done for you.

    a. positive 6 = __+6__   b. losing $5 = _____

    c. 5 degrees below 0 = _____   d. receiving $12 = _____

2. Write the **opposite** integer of each of these. The first one is done for you.

    a. negative 4 = __+4__   b. positive 10 = _____

    c. 2 floors below ground level = _____   d. winning a card game by 6 points = _____

3. Write integers to show each idea.

    a. A train that arrives 2 hours after it was scheduled: _____

    b. A package that has 3 fewer cups than it should: _____

    c. A board that's 3 inches too short: _____   d. A golf score 5 over par: _____

    e. A paycheck that doesn't cover $35 of a family's expenses: _____

    f. 30 seconds before a missile launch: _____

    g. A team that won 6 games and lost 2: _____

MASTER SKILLS
MATH 6

Comparing Integers

Comparing two integers can be confusing unless you think of them as being on a number line, as shown below. Remember that the integer farther to the right is greater. Thus, +2 is greater than –3, 0 is greater than –4 and –2 is greater than –5.

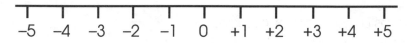

–5 –4 –3 –2 –1 0 +1 +2 +3 +4 +5

Directions: Study the number line. Then complete the following exercises.

1. Write in integers to complete the number line.

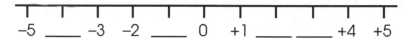

–5 ___ –3 –2 ___ 0 +1 ___ ___ +4 +5

2. Write < for "less than" or > for "greater than" to compare the integers. The first one is done for you.

−15°

a. –5 __**<**__ +5

b. +3 _____ –3

c. +2 _____ –4

d. –4 _____ –3

e. –1 _____ +3

f. –1 _____ –5

3. Write **T** for true or **F** for false. (All degrees are in Fahrenheit.)

a. +7 degrees is colder than –3 degrees.   _____

b. –14 degrees is colder than –7 degrees.   _____

c. +23 degrees is colder than –44 degrees.   _____

d. –5 degrees is colder than +4 degrees.   _____

4. Draw an **X** by the series of integers that are in order from least to greatest.

_____ +2, +3, –4

_____ –3, 0, +1

_____ –7, –4, –1

_____ –3, –4, –5

Name: _____

Adding Integers

The sum of two positive integers is a positive integer.
Thus, +4 **+** +1 = +5.
The sum of two negative integers is a negative integer.
Thus, −5 **+** −2 = −7.
The sum of a positive and a negative integer has the
sign of the integer that is farther from 0.
Thus, −6 **+** +3 = −3.
The sum of opposite integers is 0.
Thus, +2 **+** −2 = 0

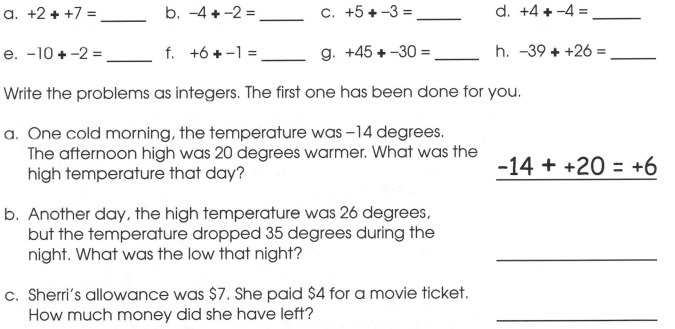

Directions: Complete the following exercises.

1. Add these integers.

    a. +2 **+** +7 = _____   b. −4 **+** −2 = _____   c. +5 **+** −3 = _____   d. +4 **+** −4 = _____

    e. −10 **+** −2 = _____   f.   +6 **+** −1 = _____   g. +45 **+** −30 = _____   h. −39 **+** +26 = _____

2. Write the problems as integers. The first one has been done for you.

    a. One cold morning, the temperature was −14 degrees.
        The afternoon high was 20 degrees warmer. What was the
        high temperature that day?

        −14 **+** +20 = +6

    b. Another day, the high temperature was 26 degrees,
        but the temperature dropped 35 degrees during the
        night. What was the low that night?   _____

    c. Sherri's allowance was $7. She paid $4 for a movie ticket.
        How much money did she have left?   _____

    d. The temperature in a meat freezer was −10 degrees, but
        the power went off and the temperature rose 6 degrees.
        How cold was the freezer then?   _____

    e. The school carnival took in $235, but it had expenses of $185.
        How much money did the carnival make after paying
        its expenses?   _____

Name: _____

Subtracting Integers

To subtract an integer, change its sign to the opposite and add it. If you are subtracting a negative integer, make it positive and add it: +4 − −6 = +4 + +6 = +10. If you are subtracting a positive integer, make it negative and add it: +8 − +2 = +8 + −2 = +6.

More examples: −5 − −8 = −5 + +8 = +3
                      +3 − +7 = +3 + −7 = −4

Directions: Complete the following exercises.

1. Before subtracting these integers, rewrite each problem. The first one has been done for you.

   −6 − −8 = ___**−6 + +8 = +2**___   +3 − −4 = _____

   +9 − +3 = _____   −1 − −7 = _____

   +7 − −5 = _____   −4 − +3 = _____

2. Write these problems as integers. The first one is done for you.

   a. The high temperature in the Arctic Circle one day was −42 degrees. The low was −67 degrees. What was the difference between the two?   **−42 − −67 = −42 + +67 = +25**

   b. At the equator one day, the high temperature was +106 degrees. The low was +85 degrees. What was the difference between the two?   _____

   c. At George's house one morning, the thermometer showed it was +7 degrees. The radio announcer said it was −2 degrees. What is the difference between the two temperatures?   _____

   d. What is the difference between a temperature of +11 degrees and a wind-chill factor of −15 degrees?   _____

   e. During a dry spell, the level of a river dropped from 3 feet above normal to 13 feet below normal. How many feet did it drop?   _____

   f. Here are the average temperatures in a meat freezer for four days: −12, −11, −14 and −9 degrees. What is the difference between the highest and lowest temperature?   _____

Name: _____

More Integers

Directions: Use the number line to help you complete the following exercises.

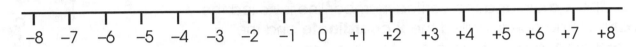

–8 –7 –6 –5 –4 –3 –2 –1 0 +1 +2 +3 +4 +5 +6 +7 +8

1. Write the following as integers:

positive 5 _____   gain of 14 _____   negative 3 _____

loss of 9 _____   positive 20 _____   negative 17 _____

2. Solve the following problems.

$+4 + +12 =$ _____ $+32 + –10 =$ _____

$–7 + +1 =$ _____ $–21 + –5 =$ _____

$+10 + –10 =$ _____ $+15 + –10 =$ _____

3. Write the integers in order from lowest to highest.

	lowest			**highest**
+4, –7, +3, 0	_____	_____	_____	_____
–18, +5, –11, +1	_____	_____	_____	_____
–8, –10, –2, –14	_____	_____	_____	_____
+2, –3, +9, –10	_____	_____	_____	_____

4. Find the difference between the following:

–22 and –17 = _____   +38 and –27 = _____

–45 and +6 = _____   –25 and –11 = _____

+4 and –4 = _____   –13 and –3 = _____

Plotting Graphs

A graph with horizontal and vertical number lines can show the location of certain points. The horizontal number line is called the **x axis**, and the vertical number line is called the **y axis**. Two numbers, called the **x coordinate** and the **y coordinate**, show where a point is on the graph.

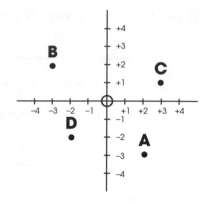

The first coordinate, x, tells how many units to the right or left of 0 the point is located. On the example graph, point A is +2, two units to the right of 0.

The second coordinate, y, tells how many units above or below 0 the point is located. On the example, point A is –3, three units below 0.

Thus, the coordinates of A are +2, –3. The coordinates of B are –3, +2. (Notice the order of the coordinates.) The coordinates of C are +3, +1; and D, –2, –2.

Directions: Study the example. Then answer these questions about the graph below.

1. What towns are at these coordinates?

+1, +3 _____

+1, –3 _____

–4, +1 _____

–2, –3 _____

–3, –2 _____

–3, +3 _____

2. What are the coordinates of these towns?

Hampton _____

Wooster _____

Beachwood _____

Middletown _____

Kirby _____

Arbor _____

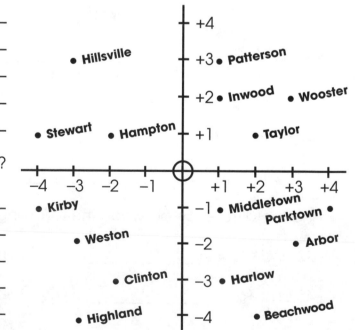

Name:_____

Ordered Pairs

Ordered pairs is another term used to describe pairs of integers used to locate points on a graph.

Directions: Complete the following exercises.

1. Place the following points on the graph, using the ordered pairs as data.

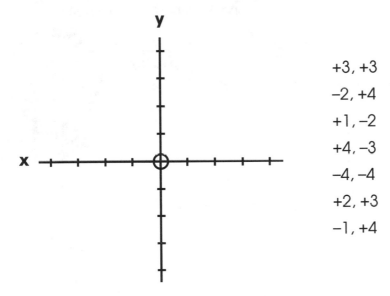

+3, +3

−2, +4

+1, −2

+4, −3

−4, −4

+2, +3

−1, +4

2. Create your own set of ordered pairs. Use your home as the center of your coordinates—zero. Let the x axis serve as East and West. The y axis will be North and South. Now select things to plot on your graph—the school, playground, grocery store, a friend's house, and so on.

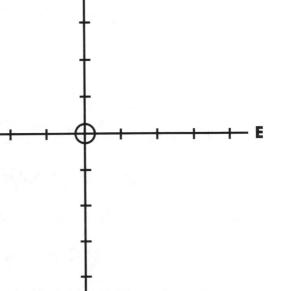

Place	Ordered pair of coordinates
School	_____
Grocery store	_____
Playground	_____
Friend's house	_____

MATH 6

Review

Directions: Complete the following exercises.

1. Write the **opposite** integers of the following:

   a. 14 degrees above 0 _____

   b. Spending $21 _____

2. Write integers to show these ideas.

   a. 4 seconds after the launch of the space shuttle _____

   b. A lake 3 feet below its usual level _____

   c. 2 days before your birthday _____

3. Write < for "less than" or > for "greater than" to compare these integers.

   −2 _____ −4   +2 _____ −3   −1 _____ +1

4. Add the integers.

   −14 + −11 = _____   −6 + +5 = _____   −7 + +7 = _____

5. Subtract the integers.

   −4 − −5 = _____   +3 − −6 = _____   +7 − +2 = _____

6. Write **T** for true or **F** for false.

   a. The x coordinate is on the horizontal number line. _____

   b. Add the x and y coordinates to find the location of a point. _____

   c. Always state the x coordinate first. _____

   d. A y coordinate of +2 would be above the horizontal number line. _____

   e. An x coordinate of +2 would be to the right of the vertical number line. _____

CERTIFICATE

Congratulations to

_____

(Your Name)

for finishing this workbook!

_____
(Date)

Glossary

Acute Angle: An angle of less than 90 degrees.

Angle: The amount of space where two lines meet.

Area: The number of square units that covers a certain space.

Average: A value that lies within a range of values.

Circumference: The distance around a circle.

Congruent Shapes: Identical geometric shapes, usually facing in different directions.

Cubic Unit: A unit with six equal sides, like a child's block.

Customary System: Measures length in inches and feet, capacity in cups and pints, weight in ounces and pounds and temperature in Fahrenheit.

Data: Gathered information (**datum**—singular).

Decimal: A number that includes a period called a **decimal point**. The digits to the right of the decimal point are a value less than one.

Denominator: The bottom number in a fraction.

Diameter: The length of a line that divides a circle in half.

Digit: A numeral.

Dividend: The number to be divided in a division problem.

Divisor: The number used to divide another number.

Equation: A number sentence in which the value on the left of the equal sign must equal the value on the right.

Equilateral Triangle: A triangle with three equal sides.

Equivalent Fractions: Fractions that name the same amount, such as $\frac{1}{2}$ and $\frac{5}{10}$.

Estimating: Using an approximate number instead of an exact one.

Expanded Notation: Writing out the value of each digit in a number.

Fraction: A number that names part of something.

Geometry: The study of lines and angles, the shapes they create and how they relate to one another.

Greatest Common Factor (GCF): The largest number that will divide evenly into a set of numbers.

Improper Fraction: A fraction that has a larger numerator than its denominator.

Integers: Numbers above or below zero: −2, −1, 0, +1, +2, and so on.

Intersecting Lines: At least two straight lines that cross each other's paths.

Isosceles Triangle: A triangle with two equal sides.

Least Common Multiple (LCM): The lowest possible multiple any pair of numbers have in common.

Line: A series of continuous points in a straight path, extending in either direction.

Line Segment: A straight line extending from one exact point to another.

Mean: The average of a group of numbers.

Median: The number in the middle when numbers are listed in order.

Metric System: Measures length in meters, capacity in liters, mass in grams and temperature in Celsius.

Mixed Number: A whole number and a fraction, such as $1\frac{3}{4}$.

Numerator: The top number in a fraction.

Obtuse Angle: An angle of more than 90 degrees.

Opposite Integers: Two integers the same distance from 0 but in different directions, such as –2 and +2.

Ordered Pairs: Another term used to describe pairs of integers used to locate points on a graph.

Parallel Lines: Lines that never get closer together or farther apart at any point.

Percent: A kind of ratio that compares a number with 100.

Perimeter: The distance around a shape formed by straight lines, such as a square or triangle.

Perpendicular Lines: Two lines that intersect each other at a 90-degree angle.

Place Value: The position of a digit in a number.

Probability: The ratio of favorable outcomes to possible outcomes in an experiment.

Proportion: A statement that two ratios are equal.

Quadrilateral: A shape with four sides and four angles.

Quotient: The answer in a division problem.

Radius: The length of a line from the center of a circle to the outside edge.

Range: The difference between the highest and lowest number in a group of numbers.

Ratio: A comparison of two quantities.

Ray: A straight line extending in one direction from one specific point.

Reciprocals: Two fractions that, when multiplied together, make 1, such as $\frac{2}{7}$ and $\frac{7}{2}$.

Right Angle: An angle of 90 degrees.

Rounding: Expressing a number to the nearest whole number, ten, thousand or other value.

Scalene Triangle: A triangle with no equal sides.

Similar Shapes: The same geometric shape in differing sizes.

Straight Angles: An angle of 180 degrees.

Symmetrical Shapes: Shapes that, when divided in half, are identical.

Vertex: The point at which two lines intersect.

Volume: The number of cubic units that fills a space.

X Axis: The horizontal number line in a plotting graph.

X Coordinate/Y Coordinate: Show where a point is on a plotting graph.

Y Axis: The vertical number line in a plotting graph.

Answer Key

Place Value

Place value is the position of a digit in a number. A digit's place in a number shows its value. Numbers left of the decimal point represent **whole numbers**. Numbers right of the decimal point represent a part, or fraction, of a whole number. These parts are broken down into tenths, hundredths, thousandths, and so on.

Example:
3,443,221.621

millions	hundred thousands	ten thousands	thousands	hundreds	tens	ones	tenths	hundredths	thousandths
3	4	4	3	2	2	1	6	2	1

←——— **Whole Numbers** ———→ | ←— **Fractions** —→

Directions: Write the following number words as numbers.

1. Three million, forty-four thousand, six hundred twenty-one   **3,044,621**
2. One million, seventy-seven   **1,000,077**
3. Nine million, six hundred thousand, one hundred two   **9,600,102**
4. Twenty-nine million, one hundred three thousand and nine tenths
    29,103,000.9
5. One million, one hundred thousand, one hundred seventy-one and thirteen hundredths   **1,100,171.13**

Directions: In each box, write the corresponding number for each place value.

1. 4,822,000.00   **[0]** hundreds
2. 55,907,003.00   **[7]** thousands
3. 190,641,225.07   **[6]** hundred thousands
4. 247,308,211.59   **[5]** tenths
5. 7,594,097.33   **[7]** millions
6. 201,480,110.01   **[4]** hundred thousands
7. 42,367,109.074.25   **[5]** hundredths

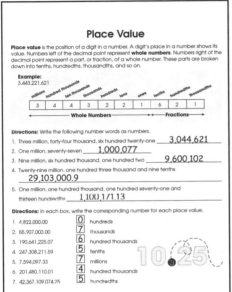

3

Place Value

The chart below shows the place value of each number.

trillions	billions	millions	thousands	ones
h t o	h t o	h t o	h t o	h t o
2	1 4 0	9 0 0	6 8 0	3 5 0

Word form: two trillion, one hundred forty billion, nine hundred million, six hundred eighty thousand, three hundred fifty

Directions: Draw a line to the correct value of each underlined digit. The first one is done for you.

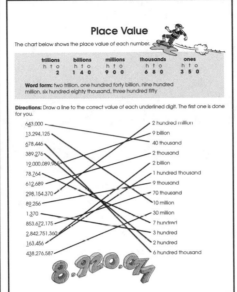

643,000 — 2 hundred million
13,294,125 — 9 billion
678,446 — 40 thousand
389,276 — 2 thousand
19,000,089,966 — 2 billion
78,764 — 1 hundred thousand
612,689 — 9 thousand
298,154,370 — 70 thousand
89,256 — 10 million
1,370 — 30 million
853,672,175 — 7 hundred
2,842,751,360 — 3 hundred
163,456 — 2 hundred
438,276,587 — 6 hundred thousand

4

Expanded Notation

Expanded notation is writing out the value of each digit in a number.

Example:
8,920,077 = 8,000,000 + 900,000 + 20,000 + 70 + 7
Word form: Eight million, nine hundred twenty thousand, seventy-seven

Directions: Write the following numbers using expanded notation.

1. 20,769,033   **20,000,000 + 700,000 + 60,000 + 9,000 + 30 + 3**
2. 1,183,541,029   **1,000,000, 000 + 100,000,000 + 80,000,000 + 3,000,000 + 500,000 + 40,000 + 1,000 + 20 + 9**
3. 776,003,091   **700,000,000 + 70,000,000 + 6,000,000 + 3,000 + 90 + 1**
4. 5,920,100,808   **5,000,000,000 + 900,000,000 + 20,000,000 + 100,000 + 800 + 8**
5. 14,141,543,760   **10,000,000,000 + 4,000,000,000 + 100,000,000 + 40,000,000 + 1,000,000 + 500,000 + 40,000 + 3,000 + 700 + 60**

Directions: Write the following numbers.

1. 700,000 + 900 + 60 + 7   **700,967**
2. 35,000,000 + 600,000 + 400 + 40 + 2   **35,600,442**
3. 12,000,000 + 700,000 + 60,000 + 4,000 + 10 + 4   **12,764,014**
4. 80,000,000,000 + 8,000,000,000 + 400,000,000 + 80,000,000 + 10,000 + 400 + 30   **88,480,010,430**
5. 4,000,000,000 + 16,000,000 + 30 + 2   **4,016,000,032**

5

Addition and Place Value

Directions: Add the problems below in which the digits with the same place value are lined up correctly. Then cross out the problems in which the digits are not lined up correctly.

Find each answer in the diagram and color that section.

yellow	blue	green	red
638 1,289 + 465 **2,392**	98 ~~328~~ ~~+ 2,755~~	4,326 82 + 699 **5,107**	589 95 + 8,526 **9,210**
579 ~~125~~ ~~+ 944~~	296 2,183 + 75 **2,554**	93,287 36 + 7,831 **101,154**	51 315 + 7,492 **7,858**
83 ~~1,298~~ ~~60~~	938 3,297 + 445 **4,680**	1,849 964 + 53 **2,866**	198 ~~72~~ ~~+ 58~~
987 ~~390~~ ~~+ 9,785~~	46 390 + 9,785 **10,221**	856 ~~452~~ ~~62~~	591 6,352 + 27 **6,970**
57 ~~7,620~~ ~~+ 464~~	773 3,118 + 74 **3,965**	64 7,430 + 338 **7,832**	919 52 + 6,835 **7,806**

6

Addition

Directions: Add the following numbers.

88 + 16 **104**	27 + 24 **51**	91 + 59 **150**	76 + 35 **111**	54 + 37 **91**	29 + 48 **77**
13 27 + 82 **122**	28 44 + 56 **128**	41 98 + 72 **211**	33 17 + 75 **125**	7 25 + 60 **92**	39 86 + 94 **219**
5,943 + 2,075 **8,018**	3,031 + 5,187 **8,218**	7,280 + 1,945 **9,225**	1,258 + 5,290 **6,548**	6,711 + 5,088 **11,799**	
9,227 1,243 + 5,012 **15,482**	8,314 702 + 7,218 **16,234**	5,693 407 + 3,920 **10,020**	2,500 4,693 + 7,055 **14,248**	3,741 9,205 + 368 **13,314**	

7

Addition

Directions: Add the following numbers in your head without writing them out.

1. 17 + 33 = **50**   2. 35 + 15 = **50**   3. 75 + 25 = **100**
4. 41 + 25 = **66**   5. 27 + 23 = **50**   6. 30 + 20 = **50**
7. 12 + 18 = **30**   8. 43 + 22 = **65**   9. 16 + 34 = **50**
10. 9 + 11 + 30 = **50**   11. 29 + 21 + 40 = **90**
12. 14 + 16 + 20 = **50**   13. 37 + 13 + 25 = **75**
14. 12 + 22 + 36 = **70**   15. 19 + 21 + 57 = **97**
16. 21 + 24 + 25 = **70**   17. 63 + 14 + 11 = **88**
18. 33 + 15 + 42 = **90**   19. 25 + 15 + 60 = **100**
20. 30 + 20 + 10 = **60**

14 + 12 + 7 + 20 + 9 + 18 = ?

8

Addition Word Problems

Directions: Solve the following addition word problems.

1. 100 students participated in a sports card show in the school gym. Brad brought his entire collection of 2,000 cards to show his friends. He had 700 football cards and 400 basketball cards. If the rest of his cards were baseball cards, how many baseball cards did he bring with him?

__900 baseball cards__

2. Refreshments were set up in one area of the gym. Hot dogs were a dollar, soda was 50 cents, chips were 35 cents and cookies were a quarter. If you purchased two of each item, how much money would you need?

__$4.20__

3. It took each student 30 minutes to set up for the card show and twice as long to put everything away. The show was open for 3 hours. How much time did each student spend on this event?

__4 ¹/₂ hours__

4. 450 people attended the card show. 55 were mothers of students, 67 were fathers, 23 were grandparents, 8 were aunts and uncles and the rest were kids. How many kids attended?

__297 kids__

5. Of the 100 students who set up displays, most of them sold or traded some of their cards. Bruce sold 75 cards, traded 15 cards and collected $225. Kevin only sold 15 cards, traded 81 cards and collected $100. Missi traded 200 cards, sold 10 and earned $35. Of those listed, how many cards were sold, how many were traded and how much money was earned?

sold __100__ traded __296__ earned $ __360__

9

Subtraction

Directions: Subtract the following numbers. When subtracting, begin on the right, especially if you need to regroup and borrow.

549 − 162 **387**	823 − 417 **406**	370 − 244 **126**	648 − 79 **569**
700 − 343 **357**	475 − 299 **176**	603 − 425 **178**	354 − 265 **89**
1,841 − 952 **889**	2,597 − 608 **1,989**	6,832 − 1,774 **5,058**	9,005 − 3,458 **5,547**
23,342 − 9,093 **14,249**	53,790 − 40,813 **12,977**	29,644 − 19,780 **9,864**	35,726 − 16,959 **18,767**
109,432 − 79,145 **30,287**	350,907 − 14,185 **336,722**	217,523 − 44,197 **173,326**	537,411 − 406,514 **130,897**

10

Subtraction

Directions: Subtract the following numbers in your head without writing them out.

1. 22 − 11 = __11__   2. 55 − 25 = __30__   3. 83 − 22 = __61__

4. 36 − 14 = __22__   5. 68 − 17 = __51__   6. 70 − 34 = __36__

7. 77 − 32 = __45__   8. 94 − 50 = __44__   9. 85 − 16 = __69__

10. 42 − 21 = __21__   11. 53 − 23 = __30__

12. 95 − 30 = __65__   13. 135 − 65 = __70__

14. 316 − 10 = __306__   15. 248 − 22 = __226__

16. 747 − 525 = __222__   17. 495 − 255 = __240__

18. 815 − 312 = __503__   19. 410 − 220 = __190__

20. 347 − 120 = __227__   21. 726 − 529 = __197__

22. 920 − 721 = __199__   23. 1,220 − 410 = __810__

24. 3,475 − 1,200 = __2,275__   25. 2,116 − 1,072 = __1,044__

26. 4,750 − 4,725 = __25__   27. 1,170 − 1,135 = __35__

28. 5,621 − 875 = __4,746__   29. 8,765 − 3,748 = __5,017__

30. 10,011 − 728 = __9,283__   31. 17,780 − 6,213 = __11,567__

32. 32,360 − 32,160 = __200__ 33. 1,000,000 − 500,000 = __500,000__

11

Subtraction Word Problems

Directions: Solve the following subtraction word problems.

1. Last year, 28,945 people lived in Mike's town. This year there are 31,889. How many people have moved in?   __2,944 people__

2. Brad earned $227 mowing lawns. He spent $168 on tapes by his favorite rock group. How much money does he have left?   __$59__

3. The school year has 180 days. Carrie has gone to 32 school days so far. How many more days does she have left?   __148 days__

4. Craig wants a skateboard that costs $128. He has saved $47. How much more does he need?   __$81__

5. To get to school, Jennifer walks 1,275 steps and Carolyn walks 2,618 steps. How many more steps does Carolyn walk than Jennifer?   __1,343 steps__

6. Amy has placed 91 of the 389 pieces in a new puzzle she purchased. How many more does she have left to finish?   __298 pieces__

7. From New York, it's 2,823 miles to Los Angeles and 1,327 miles to Miami. How much farther away is Los Angeles?   __1,496 miles__

8. Sheila read that a piece of carrot cake has 236 calories, but a piece of apple pie has 427 calories. How many calories will she save by eating the cake instead of the pie?   __191 calories__

9. Tim's summer camp costs $223, while Sam's costs $149. How much more does Tim's camp cost?   __$74__

10. Last year, the nation's budget was $45,000,000,000, but the nation spent $52,569,342,000. How much more than its budget did the nation spend?   __$ 7,569,342,000__

12

Multiplication

Directions: Multiply the following numbers. Be sure to keep the numbers aligned, and place a 0 in the ones place.

Example:	Correct	Incorrect
	55 x 15 275 550 **825**	55 x 15 275 55 **330**

1. 12 x 6 **72**	2. 44 x 9 **396**	3. 27 x 7 **189**	4. 92 x 6 **552**	5. 85 x 9 **765**
6. 78 x 24 **1,872**	7. 32 x 17 **544**	8. 19 x 46 **874**	9. 63 x 12 **756**	10. 38 x 77 **2,926**
11. 125 x 6 **750**	12. 641 x 25 **16,025**	13. 713 x 47 **33,511**	14. 586 x 45 **26,370**	15. 294 x 79 **23,226**

16. 20 x 4 x 7 = __560__   17. 9 x 5 x 11 = __495__

18. 16 x 2 x 2 = __64__   19. 7 x 3 x 6 = __126__

20. 33 x 11 x 3 = __1,089__   21. 2 x 8 x 10 = __160__

13

Multiplication Word Problems

Directions: Solve the following multiplication word problems. Remember to multiply the ones first, then the tens, then the hundreds.

Example:	1 542 x 6 2	2 542 x 6 52	542 x 6 **3,252**

1. Angela bought 6 tapes for $12 each. How much did she spend?   __$72__

2. Steve finished 9 pages of math with 24 problems on each page. How many problems did he do?   __216 problems__

3. Dana sold 27 boxes of candy for $3 each, but she thinks she may have lost some of the money. How much money should she have?   __$81__

4. Nathan rides his bike 4 miles to school every day. How far will he ride in 31 days?   __124 miles__

5. Julie swam the length of the pool 7 times. It took her 31 seconds each time. How many seconds did she swim altogether?   __217 seconds__

6. In Derek's scout group, 4 boys have earned 14 badges each. How many badges have they earned altogether?   __56 badges__

7. For a school party, 7 families sent in a dozen cookies each. How many cookies in all were sent?   __84 cookies__

8. Matt mowed 8 lawns for $11 each. Tito mowed 12 lawns for $9 each. Who made more money, and how much more did he make?   __Tito/$20__

9. The teacher needed 14 volunteers to work 3 hours each. How many hours of help did he need?   __42 hours__

10. The city's stadium, which has 14,900 seats, was sold out for 6 baseball games last summer. How many people came to those games?   __89,400 people__

14

Multiplying With Zeros

Directions: Multiply the following numbers. If a number ends with zero, you can eliminate it while calculating the rest of the answer. Then count how many zeros you took off and add them to your answer.

Example:

550	Take off 2 zeros	500	Take off 2 zeros
x 50		x 5	
27,500	Add on 2 zeros	2,500	Add on 2 zeros

1. 300 x 6	2. 400 x 7	3. 620 x 5	4. 290 x 7
1,800	**2,800**	**3,100**	**2,030**

5. 142 x 20	6. 505 x 50	7. 340 x 70	8. 600 x 60
2,840	**25,250**	**23,800**	**36,000**

9. 550 x 380	10. 290 x 150	11. 2,040 x 360	12. 8,800 x 200
209,000	**43,500**	**734,400**	**1,760,000**

13. Bruce traveled 600 miles each day of a 10-day trip. How far did he go during the entire trip? **6,000 miles**

14. 30 children each sold 20 items for the school fund-raiser. Each child earned $100 for the school. How much money did the school collect? **$2,000**

15. 10 x 40 x 2 = **800**   16. 30 x 30 x 10 = **9,000**
17. 100 x 60 x 10 = **60,000**   18. 500 x 11 x 2 = **11,000**
19. 9 x 10 x 10 = **900**   20. 7,000 x 20 x 10 = **1,400,000**

15

Division

In a division problem, the **dividend** is the number to be divided, the **divisor** is the number used to divide and the **quotient** is the answer. To check your work, multiply your answer times the divisor and you should get the dividend.

Example:

```
          130 ← quotient       Check:    130 ← quotient
divisor→ 4|520 ← dividend              x  4 ← divisor
          4                            520 ← dividend
          12
          12
          00
```

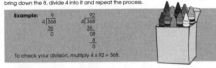

Directions: Solve the following division problems.

1. 182 3|546	2. 144 5|720	3. 229 2|458	4. 199 4|796	5. 128 7|896

6. 32 4|128	7. 94 4|376	8. 45 5|225	9. 228 3|684	10. 154 6|924

11. 19 25|475	12. 48 16|768	13. 60 14|840	14. 19 22|418	15. 33 21|693

Directions: Solve these division problems in your head. Challenge yourself for speed and accuracy.

1. 22 ÷ 2 = **11**   2. 15 ÷ 3 = **5**   3. 72 ÷ 9 = **8**
4. 36 ÷ 4 = **9**   5. 27 ÷ 9 = **3**   6. 56 ÷ 8 = **7**
7. 81 ÷ 9 = **9**   8. 42 ÷ 6 = **7**   9. 63 ÷ 9 = **7**
10. 60 ÷ 5 = **12**   11. 70 ÷ 10 = **7**   12. 98 ÷ 7 = **14**
13. 55 ÷ 5 = **11**   14. 64 ÷ 8 = **8**   15. 84 ÷ 3 = **28**

16

Division Word Problems

In the example below, 368 is being divided by 4. 4 won't divide into 3, so move over one position and divide 4 into 36. 4 goes into 36 nine times. Then multiply 4 x 9 to get 36. Subtract 36 from 36. The answer is 0, less than the divisor, so 9 is the right number. Now bring down the 8, divide 4 into it and repeat the process.

Example:

```
       9              92
   4|368          4|368
     36              36
      0              08
                      8
                      0
```

To check your division, multiply 4 x 92 = 368.

Directions: Solve the following division problems. (For some problems, you will also need to add or subtract.)

1. Kristy helped the kindergarten teacher put a total of 192 crayons into 8 boxes. How many crayons did they put into each box? **24 crayons**

2. The scout troop has to finish a 12-mile hike in 3 hours. How many miles an hour will they have to walk? **4 miles per hour**

3. At her slumber party, Shelly had 4 friends and 25 pieces of candy. If she kept 5 pieces and divided the rest among her friends, how many pieces did each friend get? **5 pieces**

4. Kenny's book has 147 pages. He wants to read the same number of pages each day and finish reading the book in 7 days. How many pages should he read each day? **21 pages**

5. Brian and 2 friends are going to share 27 marbles. How many will each person get? **9 marbles**

6. To help the school, 5 parents agreed to sell 485 tickets for a raffle. How many tickets will each person have to sell to do his/her part? **97 tickets**

7. Tim is going to weed his neighbor's garden for $3 an hour. How many hours does he have to work to make $72? **24 hours**

17

Equations

In an **equation**, the value on the left of the equal sign must equal the value on the right. Remember the order of operations: solve from left to right, multiply or divide numbers before adding or subtracting and do the operation inside parentheses first.

Example:
```
6 + 4 - 2 = 4 x 2
  10 - 2  =  8
      8   =  8
```

Directions: Write the correct operation signs in the blanks to make accurate equations.

1. (25 **+** 25) **÷** 2 = 100 **−** 75
2. (76 **−** 24) **X** 3 = 150 **X** 2
3. 140 **÷** 2 **X** 10 = 500 **+** 50 **+** 150
4. 2,100 **−** 2,000 **+** 60 = 80 **X** 2
5. 80 **−** 8 **÷** 4 = 160 **−** 160
6. 55 **X** 100 **÷** 11 = 1,000 **X** 2 **−** 4
7. 137 **+** 81 **−** 52 = 3 **X** 90
8. 3,000 **÷** 10 **÷** 10 = (600 **+** 300) **÷** 30
9. (720 **+** 20) **÷** 4 = 37 **X** 5
10. 457 **+** 43 **−** 500 = (21 **+** 40) x 0

18

Equations

Directions: Write the correct operation signs in the blanks to make accurate equations.

1. 5 **+** 5 **+** 5 = 3 **X** 5 **+** 0
2. (50 **+** 0) **X** 2 = 25 **X** 2 **X** 2
3. 28 **+** 28 **+** 2 = 2 **X** 2 **X** 4
4. (4 **X** 5) **+** 5 **+** 5 = 2 **X** 3 **X** 5
5. (25 **+** 5) **X** 2 **X** 3 = 3 **X** 6 **X** 2 **X** 5
6. (125 **X** 7) **+** 2 **+** 3 = 100 **X** 2 **X** 4 **+** 70 **+** 10
7. (100 **X** 10) **X** 5 **+** 10 = 10 **X** 5 **X** 100 **+** 10
8. 35 **+** 35 **+** 5 = 5 **X** (3 **X** 3) **+** 6
9. (60 **÷** 2) **X** 3 = 3 **X** 3 **X** 3 **X** 0 **+** 15 **+** (5 **X** 15)
10. (120 **X** 4) **+** 7 **+** 3 = (7 **X** 7) **X** (2 **X** 5)
11. 91 **+** 3 **+** 6 **X** 3 = 2 **X** 5 **X** 1 **X** 3 **X** (2 **X** 5)
12. (16 **−** 4) **X** 8 = 5 **+** 5 **X** (3 **X** 3) **+** 6
13. 10 **+** 5 **+** 5 = 4 **+** 3 **+** 3 **X** 8
14. 16 **X** 3 **+** 12 = (2 **X** 20) = (2 **X** 2) **X** 6 **+** 10 **−** (2 **X** 7)
15. 21 **+** (3 **X** 3) **−** 3 **−** 1 = 3 **÷** 1 **X** 2 **+** 20

19

Mixed Practice Word Problems

Directions: Read each word problem carefully. Eliminate insignificant information. Determine what you need to know to find the correct answer.

1. 5 cars lined up for the first race of the spring rally. The track was one-half mile long. Each car had to complete 22 laps around the track. How many miles did they travel altogether? **55 miles**

2. It took the last car 42 minutes to finish the race. The winner did it in half that time. How long did it take the winner to complete 22 laps around the track? **21 minutes**

3. During the presentation of awards, they announced that a new record had been set that day. The old record was 185 miles per hour and the new record was 217 miles per hour. How much faster was the new record? **32 miles per hour**

4. 1,200 people attended the car rally. All proceeds from the day's events were donated to a local charity. They earned the following amounts of money before expenses:

	Expenses
Admission tickets — $3,600	$400
Concession stand — $2,150	$725
Donations — $325	

How much were they able to give to charity? **$4,950.00**

5. The local boy scouts and girl scouts offered to clean up the trash after the rally. 40 children arrived to help. 17 of them could only help for 1 hour. Another 12 stayed 2 hours. Combined, it took all the children a total of 74 hours to complete the task. How many hours did each of the other scouts have to help? **3 hours**

20

Find the Mean

Mean (the average group of numbers) is a term frequently used for **average** (a value that lies within a range of values). To find the mean, add the numbers, then divide by the number of items.

Directions: Match each mean with the correct number by writing the corresponding letter.

Example: 10 + 20 + 30 = 60   60 ÷ 3 = 20   Mean = 20

		Mean	
1. 25, 75, 215		E	A. 775
2. 170, 220, 150		I	B. 555
3. 390, 465, 810		B	C. 39
4. 12, 16, 22, 18, 17		J	D. 1,560
5. 500, 800, 1,200, 600		A	E. 105
6. 78, 340, 290, 188		H	F. 2,463
7. 5, 19, 76, 43, 52		C	G. 510
8. 4,020, 1,368, 2,001		F	H. 224
9. 640, 935, 1,306, 3,359		D	I. 180
10. 852, 316, 701, 468, 213		G	J. 17

Find the mean age of all your family members. Include grandparents, aunts, uncles and cousins.

21

Averaging

To find an average, add the numbers, then divide by the number of items.

Example: Test scores of 89, 74, and 92:

```
  89        85
  74     3)255
+ 92        24
 255        15
            15
             0
```

Your average score is **85**.

Directions: Solve each word problem below. (Do your adding and dividing on another sheet of paper.)

1. One bear at the zoo weighs 524 pounds, one weighs 756 pounds and one weighs 982 pounds. What is the average of their total weight?   **754 lbs.**

2. Three new cars cost $10,100, $7,800 and $12,400. What is the average cost?   **$10,100**

3. Paul's school has 684 students, Nicole's has 841 and Kurt's has 497. What is the average number of students at these three schools?   **674 students**

4. One street in our neighborhood has 43 houses, one has 26, one has 18 and one has 37. What is the average number of houses per street?   **31 houses**

5. Lynn has 365 stickers in her collection, Bridget has 343, Karen has 219 and Liz has 141. What is the average number of stickers?   **267 stickers**

6. Four libraries each have this many books: 10,890; 14,594; 9,786; 12,754. What is the average number of books for the libraries?   **12,006 books**

7. Doug found 5 different candy bars with these prices: 45, 65, 90, 85 and 75 cents. What was the average price?   **72¢**

8. Four neighboring towns each have this many residents: 6,033; 4,589; 5,867; 1,239. What is the average population of these towns?   **4,432**

9. The weekly grocery bill for Jamie's family totaled these amounts for the past 6 weeks: $88, $119, $97, $104, $86 and $112. What does her family spend on groceries, on average?   **$101**

22

Rounding and Estimating

Rounding is expressing a number to the nearest whole number, ten, thousand or other value. **Estimating** is using an approximate number instead of an exact one. When rounding a number, we say a country has 98,000,000 citizens instead of 98,347,425. We can round off numbers to the nearest whole number, the nearest hundred or the nearest million—whatever is appropriate.

Here are the steps: 1) Decide where you want to round off the number. 2) If the digit to the right is less than 5, leave the digit at the rounding place unchanged. 3) If the digit to the right is 5 or more, increase the digit at the rounding place by 1.

Examples: 587 rounded to the nearest hundred is 600.
535 rounded to the nearest hundred is 500.
21,897 rounded to the nearest thousand is 22,000.
21,356 rounded to the nearest thousand is 21,000.

When we estimate numbers, we use rounded, approximate numbers instead of exact ones.

Example: A hamburger that costs $1.49 and a drink that costs $0.79 total about $2.30 ($1.50 plus $0.80).

Directions: Use rounding and estimating to find the answers to these questions. You may have to add, subtract, multiply or divide.

1. Debbi is having a party and wants to fill 11 cups from a 67-ounce bottle of pop. About how many ounces should she pour into each cup?   **6 ounces**

2. Tracy studied 28 minutes every day for 4 days. About how long did she study in all?   **120 minutes**

3. About how much does this lunch cost? $1.19 $0.39 $0.49   **$2.00**

4. The numbers below show how long Frank spent studying last week. Estimate how many minutes he studied for the whole week.
Monday: 23 minutes Tuesday: 37 minutes Wednesday: 38 minutes
Thursday: 12 minutes   **110 minutes**

5. One elephant at the zoo weighs 1,417 pounds and another one weighs 1,789 pounds. About how much heavier is the second elephant?   **400 lbs.**

6. If Tim studied a total of 122 minutes over 4 days, about how long did he study each day?   **30 minutes**

7. It's 549 miles to Dover and 345 miles to Albany. About how much closer is Albany?   **200 miles**

23

Rounding

Directions: Round off each number, then estimate the answer. You can use a calculator to find the exact answer.

Round to the nearest ten.

	Estimate	**Actual Answer**
1. 86 + 9 =	10	9.56
2. 237 + 488 =	730	725
3. 49 × 11 =	500	539
4. 309 + 412 =	720	721
5. 625 − 218 =	410	407

Round to the nearest hundred.

6. 790 − 70 =	700	720
7. 690 + 70 =	7	9.86
8. 2,177 − 955 =	1,200	1,222
9. 4,792 + 3,305 =	8,100	8,097
10. 5,210 × 90 =	520,00	468,900

Round to the nearest thousand.

11. 4,078 + 2,093 =	6,000	6,171
12. 5,525 − 3,065 =	3,000	2,460
13. 6,047 + 2,991 =	2	2.02
14. 1,913 × 4,216 =	8,000,000	8,065,208
15. 7,227 + 8,449 =	15,000	15,676

24

Review

Directions: Solve the following problems. Round off answers to the nearest hundredth where necessary.

1. Write these numbers in words:
a. 2,240 **Two thousand, two hundred forty**
b. 4,873,189 **Four million, eight hundred seventy-three thousand, one hundred eighty-nine**

2. Sara sold 23 glasses of lemonade for 15 cents a glass. Beth sold 32 glasses of lemonade for 12 cents a glass. Who made more money and how much more did she make?   **Beth/39¢**

3. Kent had 4 Superman comic books and 6 times as many Batman comic books. How many did he have altogether?   **28 comic books**

4. Cheryl bought 2 packages of beads with 425 in each package. She divided them equally among herself and 4 other people. How many beads did each person receive?   **170 beads**

5. Four of Eric's guppies had 27 babies each. The next morning he could find only 58 baby guppies. How many babies were missing?   **50 guppies**

6. Mindy made 2 batches of cookies. Each batch had 48 cookies. Then she gave all 27 kids in her class 3 cookies each. (She also ate 3 herself.) How many cookies were left over for her family?   **12 cookies**

7. Ronnie's family bought a new car that cost $9,000. They made a down payment of $1,500. If they pay $250 a month, how many months will it take to pay for the car?   **30 months**

8. Estimate how many hours are in a week.   **168 hours**

9. Round off these numbers:
a. To the nearest hundred: 4,328 **4,300**   7,679 **7,700**
b. To the nearest thousand: 4,328 **4,000**   7,679 **8,000**
c. To the nearest million: 245,763,132 **246,000,000**

25

Review

Directions: Solve the following problems.

1. 43 28 +92 163	2. 1,720 8,341 +2,199 12,260	3. 485 −317 168	4. 7,241 −4,355 2,886

5. 23 + 24 + 20 = 67	6. 49 + 11 + 40 = 100	
7. 2,400 − 1,250 = 1,150	8. 3,650 − 2,000 = 1,650	

9. 89 × 7 623	10. 342 × 36 12,312	

11. 3)627 290	12. 12)816 68	
13. 16 × 3 = 48	14. 42 ÷ 7 = 6	
15. 24 × 2 = 48	16. 96 ÷ 3 = 32	
17. 80 × 11 = 880	18. 84 ÷ 6 = 14	

19. 213 × 50 10,650	20. 45)540 12

26

Review

Directions: Estimate the following problems by rounding to the nearest ten, hundred or thousand.

1. 53 x 11 = __600__   2. 955 − 538 = __500__   3. 96 x 218 = __20,000__

4. 342 + 386 = __700__   5. 7,922 + 415 = __20__   6. 663 + 774 = __1,500__

7. 6,444 + 37 = __150__   8. 533 x 897 = __450,000__   9. 695 − 279 = __400__

10. Jerod had 123 cars in his collection. He offered to share them with 6 of his friends. About how many cars should Jerod give each person? __20 cars__

11. Emily wanted to buy lunch for herself, her mother and her sister. Each wanted a hamburger at $2.47 each, fries at $0.98 each, a salad at $1.45 each and her sister wanted a milkshake at $1.33. Emily had $16. Did she have enough money to treat everyone? __No__

12. Jonathan drove 61 miles on Monday, 23 miles on Tuesday, 46 miles on Wednesday, 72 miles on Thursday and only 9 miles on Friday. Did he drive more or less than 215 miles altogether? __Less__

13. Brittany collected dolls from all over the world. She had 21 from Spain, 43 from Canada, 65 from England, 24 from the United States and 13 from Japan. She needed 150 to enter in the doll show. Did she have enough? __Yes__

27

Decimals

A **decimal** is a number that includes a period called a **decimal point**. The digits to the right of the decimal point are a value less than one.

one whole   one tenth   one hundredth

The place value chart below helps explain decimals.

hundreds	tens	ones	tenths	hundredths	thousandths
6	3	2	.	4		
	4	7	.	0	5	
		8	.	0	0	9

A decimal is read as "and." The first number, 632.4, is read as "six hundred thirty-two and four tenths." The second number, 47.05, is read as "forty-seven and five hundredths." The third number, 8.009, is read as "eight and nine thousandths."

Directions: Write the decimals shown below. Two have been done for you.

1. __1.4__   2. __1.16__   3. __1.78__

4. six and five tenths __6.5__

5. twenty-two and nine tenths __22.9__

6. thirty-six and fourteen hundredths __36.14__

7. forty-seven hundredths __0.47__

8. one hundred six and four tenths __106.4__

9. seven and three hundredths __7.03__

10. one tenth less than 0.6 __0.5__

11. one hundredth less than 0.34 __0.33__

12. one tenth more than 0.2 __0.3__

28

Adding and Subtracting Decimals

When adding or subtracting decimals, place the decimal points under each other. That way, you add tenths to tenths, for example, not tenths to hundredths. Add or subtract beginning on the right, as usual. Carry or borrow numbers in the same way. Adding 0 to the end of decimals does not change their value, but sometimes makes them easier to add and subtract.

Examples:

```
  39.40      0.064      3.56      6.83
+  6.81    + 0.470    -  .09    - 2.14
 46.21      0.534      3.47      4.69
```

Directions: Solve the following problems.

1. Write each set of numbers in a column and add them.

   a. 2.56 + 0.6 + 76 = __79.16__

   b. 93.5 + 23.06 + 1.45 = __118.01__

   c. 3.23 + 91.34 + 0.85 = __95.42__

2. Write each pair of numbers in a column and subtract them.

   A. 7.89 − 0.56 = __7.33__   B. 34.56 − 6.04 = __28.52__   C. 7.6 − 3.24 = __4.36__

3. In a relay race, Alice ran her part in 23.6 seconds, Cindy did hers in 24.7 seconds and Erin took 20.09 seconds. How many seconds did they take altogether? __68.39 seconds__

4. Although Erin ran her part in 20.09 seconds today, yesterday it took her 21.55 seconds. How much faster was she today? __1.46 seconds__

5. Add this grocery bill: potatoes—$3.49; milk—$2.09; bread—$0.99; apples—$2.30 __$8.87__

6. A yellow coat cost $47.59, and a blue coat cost $36.79. How much more did the yellow coat cost? __$10.80__

7. A box of Oat Boats cereal has 14.6 ounces. A box of Sugar Circles has 17.85 ounces. How much more cereal is in the Sugar Circles box? __3.25 ounces__

8. The Oat Boats cereal has 4.03 ounces of sugar in it. Sugar Circles cereal has only 3.76 ounces. How much more sugar is in a box of Oats Boats? __0.27 ounces__

29

Adding and Subtracting Decimals

Directions: Add or subtract the following problems.

```
1.   53.5        2.    0.05      3.   25.4       4.   16.28
     20.07            0.83           16.09            2.43
   + 1.85          + 1.04         + 31.62         + 11.11
    75.42            1.92           73.11           29.82

5.   14.29        6.   48.90      7.   29.62      8.   84.13
   - 11.17          - 16.49         - 19.55         - 15.25
     3.12            32.41           10.07           68.88

9.    4.32       10.    1.46
     17.1              8.2
    206.06             3.003
  + 20.121          + 10.0
    247.601           22.663

11. 146.023      12. 275.486
   - 37.105         - 75.5
    108.918          199.986
```

13. The principal organized the creation of a flower garden in front of the school. She purchased 50 daffodils for $23.50, 25 geraniums for $17.75 and 3 rose bushes for $4.00 each. How much did she spend on flowers altogether? __$53.25__

14. In order to complete the project, she would also need topsoil at $10.75 per bag, a shovel at $5.25 each, fertilizer at $3.50 per bag and mulch at $4.15 per bag. She bought two of everything. She only had $100 to spend for this entire project. How much money, if any, did she have left? __$52.70__

30

Mulitplying Decimals by Two-Digit Numbers

To multiply by a 2-digit number, just repeat the same steps. In the example below, first multiply 4 times 9, 4 times 5 and 4 times 3. Then multiply 2 times 9, 2 times 5 and 2 times 3. You may want to place a 0 in the ones place to make sure this answer, 718, is one digit to the left. Now add 1,436 + 7,180 to get the final answer.

Example:

```
  359      359      359      359       359       359
x  24    x  24    x  24    x  24     x  24     x  24
   6        36     1,436    1,436     1,436     1,436
                              80       180      7,180
                                                8,616
```

When one or both numbers in a multiplication problem have decimals, check to see how many digits are right of the decimal. Then place the decimal the same number of places to the left in the answer. Here's how the example above would change if it included decimals:

```
   35.9        3.59
 x 0.24      x  24
  8.616       86.16
```

The first example has one digit to the right of the decimal in 35.9 and two more in 0.24, so the decimal point is placed three digits to the left in the answer: 8.616. The second example has two digits to the right of the decimal in 3.59 and none in 24, so the decimal point is placed two digits to the left in the answer: 86.16. (Notice that you do not have to line up the decimals in a multiplication problem.)

Directions: Solve the following problems.

1. Jennie wants to buy 3 T-shirts that cost $15.99 each. How much will they cost altogether? __$47.97__

2. Steve is making $3.75 an hour packing groceries. How much will he make in 8 hours? __$30__

3. Justin made 36 cookies and sold them all at the school carnival for $0.75 each. How much money did he make? __$27__

4. Last year, the carnival made $467. This year it made 2.3 times as much. How much money did the carnival make this year? __$1,074.10__

5. Troy's car will go 21.8 miles on a gallon of gasoline. His motorcycle will go 1.7 times as far. How far will his motorcycle travel on one gallon of gas? __37.06 miles__

31

Multiplying Decimals With Zeros

The placement of the decimal is the same even if the numbers you're multiplying have zeros in them. As before, count the digits right of the decimal in the numbers you're multiplying and place the decimal the same number of places to the left in the answer.

Examples:

```
  0.87      0.45
x  0.4    x  0.9
 0.348     0.405
```

Directions: Solve the following problems.

```
1.    1.5      2.   0.67      3.  1.406     4.   6.01      5.   103
    x 0.2        x 0.5         x  0.5       x 1.40        x 0.2
     0.3         0.335        0.703         8.414         20.6

6.    4.0      7.   1.2       8.  3.04      9.   2.05     10.  4.02
    x 0.5        x 0.05        x 0.25       x  0.3        x 0.7
      2          0.06          0.76         0.615         2.814

11.  7.02     12.  60.9      13. 80.5      14.  109      15.   50
    x 0.65       x  0.3        x 0.2       x 0.5        x 0.25
    4.563        18.27         16.1         54.5         12.5
```

32

Multiplying Decimals

In some problems, you may need to add zeros in order to place the decimal point correctly.

Examples:	0.34	0.0067	0.046
	x 0.08	x 4	x 0.07
	0.0272	0.0268	0.00322

Directions: Solve the following problems.

1.	0.15	2.	0.67	3.	7.3	4.	3.59	5.	0.061
	x 0.02		x 0.08		x 0.06		x 0.08		x 0.014
	0.003		0.0536		0.438		0.2872		0.000854

6.	7.10	7.	5.05	8.	8.75	9.	0.0647	10.	3.62
	x 0.042		x 0.08		x 0.067		x 0.3		x 0.003
	0.2982		0.404		0.58625		0.01941		0.01086

11.	1.07	12.	3.03	13.	0.02	14.	0.501	15.	0.321
	x 0.05		x 0.07		x 0.02		x 0.03		x 0.09
	0.0535		0.2121		0.0004		0.01503		0.02889

16. The players and coaches gathered around for refreshments after the soccer game. Of the 30 people there, 0.50 of them had fruit drinks, 0.20 of them had fruit juice and 0.30 of them had soft drinks. How many people had each type of drink?

fruit drink	15
fruit juice	6
soft drink	9

33

Dividing Decimals by Two-Digit Numbers

Dividing by a 2-digit divisor (34 in the example below) is very similar to dividing by a 1-digit divisor. In this example, 34 will divide into 78 twice. Then multiply 34 x 2 to get 68. Subtract 68 from 78. The answer is 10, which is smaller than the divisor, so 2 was the right number. Now bring down the next 8. 34 goes into 108 three times. Continue dividing as with a 1-digit divisor.

Example:	2	23	232
	34)7,888	34)7,888	34)7,888
	68	68	68
	10	108	108
		102	102
		6	68
			68
			0

To check your division, multiply: 34 x 232 = 7,888.

When the dividend has a decimal, place the decimal point for the answer directly above the decimal point in the dividend.

Examples:	3.6	8.92
	14)50.4	34)303.28

Directions: Solve the following problems.

	0.13	0.81	4.12	1.16	2.145
1. 56)7.28	2. 23)18.63	3. 62)255.44	4. 71)82.36	5. 4)8.580

6. If socks cost $8.97 for 3 pairs, how much does one pair cost? $2.99

7. If candy bars are 6 for $2.58, how much is one candy bar? $0.43

8. You buy a bike for $152.25 and agree to make 21 equal payments. How much will each payment be? $7.25

9. You and two friends agree to spend several hours loading a truck. The truck driver gives you $36.75 to share. How much will each person get? $12.25

10. You buy 14 hamburgers and the bill comes to $32.06. How much did each hamburger cost? $2.29

34

Working With Decimals

Directions: Solve the following problems.

1.	0.79	2.	840	3.	6.53	4.	0.724	5.	1.92
	x 3.2		x 0.25		x 0.06		x 0.04		x 2.3
	2.528		210		0.3918		0.02896		4.416

	3.6	2.34	12.61	2.42	0.81
6. 6)21.6	7. 4)9.36	8. 50)630.50	9. 25)60.50	10. 55)44.55

11. Ice-cream cones are on special at $1.29 for a double scoop. If you buy 3 of them, how much will you need to pay? $3.87

12. Each cone has 2.5 ounces of ice cream on it. How much ice cream is needed to serve 100 cones? 250 ounces

13. If ice cream sells for $10.25 for 1 gallon, how much would 0.5 gallon cost? $5.13

14. The ice-cream shop sells approximately 1,500 cones per week. How many does it sell in one day? 214 cones

35

Dividing With Zeros

Sometimes you have a remainder in division problems. You can add a decimal point and zeros to the dividend and keep dividing until you have the answer.

Example:	49	49.64
	25)1,241	25)1,241.00
	100	100
	241	241
	225	225
	16	160
		150
		100
		100
		0

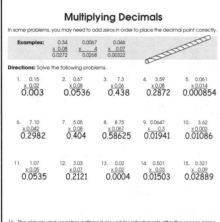

Directions: Solve the following problems.

	1.25	28.75	61.5	73.25	136.6
1. 2)2.5	2. 4)115	3. 12)738	4. 8)586	5. 3)415

6. Susie's grandparents sent her a check for $130 to share with her 7 brothers and sisters. How much will each of the 8 children get if the money is divided evenly? $16.25

7. A vendor had 396 balloons to sell and 16 workers. How many balloons should each worker sell in order to sell out? 24.75 balloons

8. Eight of the workers turned in a total of $753. How much did each worker collect if he/she sold the same number of items? 94.125 or $94.13

9. A total of 744 tickets were collected from 15 amusement ride operators on the first day of the fair. If each ride required one ticket per person, and they each collected the same number of tickets, how many people rode each ride? 49.6

Do you think that was possible? Why? No. You cannot divide a person.

10. Five people were hired to clean up the area after the fair closed. They turned in a bill for 26 hours of labor. How many hours did each person work? 5.2

36

Dividing With Zeros

Sometimes you need a zero to hold a place in the answer. In the first example below, 7 goes into 21 three times. But 7 can't be divided into 2, the next number in the dividend, so place a 0 above the 2 in the dividend. Then bring down the next number in the dividend, 8, and continue dividing.

Examples:	304	106	200.5
	7)2,128	6)636	4)802.0
	21	6	8
	028	036	0020
	28	36	20
	0	0	0

Directions: Solve the following problems, adding zeros where necessary. Check each answer by multiplying the divisor by the answer to get the dividend.

	50.2	20.25	306	40.75	904
1. 5)251	2. 16)324	3. 8)2,448	4. 8)326	5. 57)51,528

	205	253.75	1004	642.56	400.5
6. 7)1,435	7. 4)1,015	8. 5)5,020	9. 25)16,064	10. 60)24,030

11. Jimmy had 155 small pieces of candy to share with 4 of his friends. If they divide the candy evenly among the 5 children, how much will each child get? 31 pieces

12. For an art project, 5 boys divided up 530 beads. How many beads did they each get? 106 beads

13. If 8 packs of gum cost $8.48, how much did each pack cost? $1.06

37

Dividing Decimals by Decimals

When a divisor has a decimal, eliminate it before dividing. If there is one digit right of the decimal in the divisor, multiply the divisor and dividend by 10. If there are two digits right of the decimal in the divisor, multiply the divisor and dividend by 100.

Multiply the divisor and dividend by the same number whether or not the dividend has a decimal. The goal is to have a divisor with no decimal.

Examples:	2.3)89 x 10 = 23)890	4.11)67.7 x 100 = 411)6,770
	4.9)35.67 x 10 = 49)356.7	0.34)789 x 100 = 34)78,900

After removing the decimal from the divisor, work the problem in the usual way.

Directions: Solve the following problems.

	2.9	62	4.400	0.69
1. 3.5)10.15	2. 6.7)415.4	3. 0.21)924	4. 73)50.37

5. The body can burn only 0.00015 of an ounce of alcohol an hour. If an average-sized person has 1 drink, his/her blood alcohol concentration (BAC) is 0.0003. How many hours will it take his/her body to remove that much alcohol from the blood? 2 hrs.

6. If the same person has 2 drinks in 1 hour, his/her blood alcohol concentration increases to 0.0006. Burning 0.00015 ounce of alcohol an hour, how many hours will it take that person's body to burn off 2 drinks? 4 hrs.

7. If someone has 3 drinks in 1 hour, the blood alcohol concentration rises to 0.0009. At 0.00015 an hour, how many hours will it take to burn off 3 drinks? 6 hrs.

8. After a drunk driving conviction, the driver's car insurance can increase by as much as $2,000. Still, this is only 0.57 of the total cost of the conviction. What is the total cost, in round numbers? $3,509

9. In Ohio in 1986, about 335 fatal car crashes were alcohol related. That was 0.47 of the total number of fatal car crashes. About how many crashes were there altogether, in round numbers? 713 crashes

38

Panel 39 — Review

Directions: Solve the following problems.

1. Write these numbers as decimals:
   a. thirty-six and seventy-four hundredths — **36.74**
   b. twenty-nine and four tenths — **29.04**
   c. sixty-five hundredths — **0.65**
   d. one tenth less than 0.7 — **0.8**
2. Blue Bridge is 0.45 miles long, while Yellow Bridge is 1.23 miles long. How much longer is Yellow Bridge than Blue Bridge? — **0.78 miles**
3. Chris spent 23.6 minutes studying for a history test, 17.54 minutes doing math problems and 19.4 minutes writing a short story. How many minutes did Chris spend on homework altogether? — **60.54 minutes**
4. Sean's truck can carry 1,289.5 pounds. How many pounds would it hold if it were 0.75 full? — **967.13 lbs.**
5. Sherri has a picture that is 3.5 inches wide. She plans to enlarge it 2.5 times. How wide would it be then? — **8.75 inches**
6. A computer printer takes 0.025 of a second to print one letter. How long would it take to print the word technology? — **0.25 second**
7. Statistics show that 0.97 of the 6,500,000 alcoholics in the U.S. are ordinary people, not "bums," as some think. How many alcoholics in the U.S. are ordinary people? — **6,305,000**
8. At Super Store, a package of blank tapes costs $5.96 for 4 tapes. Sav-Here sells a package of 6 tapes for $7.20. How much could you save on each blank tape at Sav-Here? — **$0.29**
9. If you wanted to divide 8.5 pounds of sugar equally into 4 bowls, exactly how many pounds should you place in each bowl? — **2.13 lbs. (or 2.125 lbs.)**
10. Ten workers picked 832 oranges in 8 minutes. How many did they pick every minute, on average? — **104 oranges**

39

Panel 40 — Review

Directions: Follow the instructions below.

Add.

1.	2.	3.	4.
5.23	49.40	92.5	81.45
+ 6.07	+ 3.81	+ 7.45	2.37
11.30	**53.21**	**99.95**	+ 5.10
			88.92

5. Brian bought the following items: shoes for $79.00, jeans for $45.50 and a hat for $17.95. How much did he spend altogether? — **$142.45**

Subtract.

1.	2.	3.	4.
5.6	24.36	87.68	1.03
− 2.34	− 6.07	− 46.70	− 0.97
3.26	**18.29**	**40.98**	**0.06**

5. Liz used a $20 bill for a purchase of $14.98. How much change should she get back? — **$5.02**

Multiply.

1.	2.	3.	4.
4.82	61.08	15.3	145.06
x 34	x 1.5	x 2.7	x 0.43
163.88	**91.62**	**41.31**	**62.3758**

5. Greg bought 3 soccer balls for $47.50 each. How much did he spend altogether? — **$142.50**

Divide.

1. 4)52.6 → **13.15**
2. 18)93.6 → **5.2**
3. 45)5.13 → **0.114**
4. 40)70.6 → **1.765**

5. Krysti selected 12 CD's at the music store, all at the same cost. Her total bill was $87. How much did she pay for each CD? — **$7.25**

40

Panel 41 — Decimals and Fractions

A **fraction** is a number that names part of something. The top number in a fraction is called the **numerator**. The bottom number is called the **denominator**. Since a decimal also names part of a whole number, every decimal can also be written as a fraction. For example, 0.1 is read as "one tenth" and can also be written $\frac{1}{10}$. The decimal 0.56 is read as "fifty-six hundredths" and can also be written $\frac{56}{100}$.

Examples:
$0.7 = \frac{7}{10}$ $0.34 = \frac{34}{100}$ $0.761 = \frac{761}{1,000}$ $\frac{5}{10} = 0.58$ $\frac{58}{100} = 0.58$ $\frac{729}{1,000} = 0.729$

Even a fraction that doesn't have 10, 100 or 1,000 as the denominator can be written as a decimal. Sometimes you can multiply both the numerator and denominator by a certain number so the denominator is 10, 100 or 1,000. (You can't just multiply the denominator. That would change the amount of the fraction.)

Examples:
$\frac{3 \times 2}{5 \times 2} = \frac{6}{10} = 0.6$ $\frac{4 \times 4}{25 \times 4} = \frac{16}{100} = 0.16$

Other times, divide the numerator by the denominator.

Examples:
$\frac{3}{4} = 4)3.00 = 0.75$ $\frac{5}{8} = 8)5.000 = 0.625$

Directions: Follow the instructions below.

1. For each square, write a decimal and a fraction to show the part that is colored. The first one has been done for you.

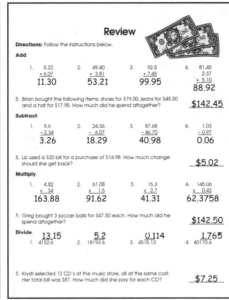

a. $\frac{25}{100}$ **0.25**   b. $\frac{60}{100}$ **0.60**   c. $\frac{32}{100}$ **0.32**

2. Change these decimals to fractions.
   a. $0.6 = \frac{6}{10}$ b. $0.54 = \frac{54}{100}$ c. $0.751 = \frac{751}{1,000}$ d. $0.73 = \frac{73}{100}$ e. $0.592 = \frac{592}{1,000}$ f. $0.2 = \frac{2}{10}$

3. Change these fractions to decimals. If necessary, round off the decimals to the nearest hundredth.
   a. $\frac{3}{10} = 0.3$ b. $\frac{89}{100} = 0.89$ c. $\frac{473}{1,000} = 0.473$ d. $\frac{4}{5} = 0.8$ e. $\frac{35}{50} = 0.7$
   f. $\frac{7}{9} = .78$ g. $\frac{1}{3} = 0.33$ h. $\frac{23}{77} = 0.30$ i. $\frac{12}{63} = 0.19$ j. $\frac{4}{16} = 0.25$

41

Panel 42 — Equivalent Fractions and the Lowest Term

Equivalent fractions name the same amount. For example, $\frac{1}{2}$, $\frac{4}{8}$, and $\frac{36}{72}$ are exactly the same amount. (And they are all written as the same decimal: 0.5.) To find an equivalent fraction, multiply the numerator and denominator of any fraction by the same number.

Examples: $\frac{3 \times 3}{4 \times 3} = \frac{9}{12}$ $\frac{4 \times 4}{12 \times 4} = \frac{36}{48}$ Thus, $\frac{3}{4}$, $\frac{9}{12}$ and $\frac{36}{48}$ are all equivalent fractions.

Most of the time, we want fractions in their lowest terms. It's easier to work with $\frac{3}{4}$ than $\frac{36}{48}$. To find a fraction's lowest term, instead of multiplying both parts of a fraction by the same number, divide.

Examples: $\frac{36 \div 12}{48 \div 12} = \frac{3}{4}$ The lowest term for $\frac{36}{48}$ is $\frac{3}{4}$.

If the numerator and denominator in a fraction can't be divided by any number, the fraction is in its lowest term. The fractions below are in their lowest terms.

Examples: $\frac{34}{61}$ $\frac{3}{5}$ $\frac{7}{9}$ $\frac{53}{90}$ $\frac{78}{83}$ $\frac{3}{8}$

Directions: Follow the instructions below.

1. Write two equivalent fractions for each fraction. Make sure you multiply the numerator and denominator by the same number. The first one is done for you.
   a. $\frac{1 \times 3}{2 \times 3} = \frac{3}{6}$ $\frac{1 \times 4}{2 \times 4} = \frac{4}{8}$ b. $\frac{2 \times 2}{4 \times 2} = \frac{4}{8}$ $\frac{2 \times 3}{4 \times 3} = \frac{6}{12}$
   c. $\frac{3 \times 2}{5 \times 2} = \frac{6}{10}$ $\frac{3 \times 3}{5 \times 3} = \frac{9}{15}$ d. $\frac{8 \times 2}{9 \times 2} = \frac{16}{18}$ $\frac{8 \times 3}{9 \times 3} = \frac{24}{27}$

2. Find the lowest terms for each fraction. Make sure your answers can't be divided by any other numbers. The first one is done for you.
   a. $\frac{2 \div 2}{36 \div 2} = \frac{1}{18}$ b. $\frac{12 \div 1}{25 \div 1} = \frac{12}{25}$ c. $\frac{12 \div 4}{16 \div 4} = \frac{3}{4}$
   d. $\frac{3 \div 3}{9 \div 3} = \frac{1}{3}$ e. $\frac{25 \div 5}{45 \div 5} = \frac{5}{9}$ f. $\frac{11 \div 11}{44 \div 11} = \frac{1}{4}$

42

Panel 43 — Greatest Common Factor

The **greatest common factor (GCF)** is the largest number that will divide evenly into a set of numbers. In the example, both numbers can be divided evenly by 2 and 4; therefore, 4 is the greatest common factor.

Example: 12 and 20   2, 4 (can be divided evenly into both numbers)
4 (greatest common factor)

Directions: Circle the greatest common factor for each pair of numbers.

1. 56 and 72	6	10	**(8)**	2
2. 45 and 81	7	5	**(9)**	3
3. 28 and 49	**(7)**	11	4	6
4. 10 and 35	3	**(5)**	9	7
5. 42 and 30	4	2	5	**(6)**
6. 121 and 33	12	9	4	**(11)**
7. 96 and 48	**(48)**	15	6	3
8. 12 and 132	2	10	**(12)**	9
9. 108 and 27	14	9	3	**(27)**
10. 44 and 32	**(4)**	6	8	10
11. 16 and 88	12	2	**(8)**	5
12. 72 and 144	9	11	7	**(72)**

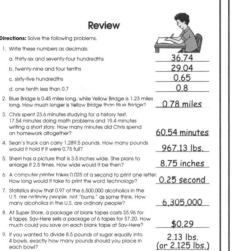

43

Panel 44 — Least Common Multiple

The **least common multiple (LCM)** is the lowest possible multiple any pair of numbers have in common.

Examples: 2 and 4
The least common multiple is 4, because 4 is a multiple for each number and it is the lowest possible.

6 and 7
Multiples of 6 are 6, 12, 18, 24, 30, 36, 42.
Multiples of 7 are 7, 14, 21, 28, 35, 42.
42 is the lowest multiple that 6 and 7 have in common.

Directions: Find the least common multiple for each pair of numbers.

1. 7 and 8 = **56**
2. 2 and 3 = **6**
3. 11 and 4 = **44**
4. 5 and 3 = **15**
5. 7 and 2 = **14**
6. 9 and 4 = **36**
7. 2 and 6 = **6**
8. 10 and 3 = **30**
9. 7 and 5 = **35**
10. 9 and 6 = **18**
11. 12 and 8 = **24**
12. 15 and 3 = **15**

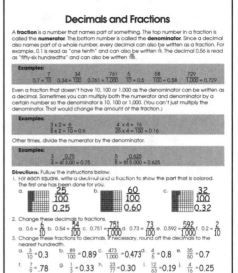

44

Comparing Decimals and Fractions

The symbol **>** means greater than. The number on its left is greater than that on its right. The symbol **<** means less than. The number on its left is less than that on its right. An equal sign, **=**, shows the same value on each side.

Directions: Use the sign >, = or < to make each statement true.

1. 0.4 $<$ $\frac{2}{3}$ 2. 1.25 $<$ $\frac{3}{2}$

3. 0.7 $<$ $\frac{4}{5}$ 4. 0.68 $<$ $\frac{5}{7}$

5. 0.1 $>$ $\frac{1}{12}$ 6. 0.45 $<$ $\frac{1}{2}$

7. 0.75 $>$ $\frac{3}{8}$ 8. 0.6 $<$ $\frac{5}{8}$

9. 0.54 $>$ $\frac{2}{5}$ 10. 0.8 $>$ $\frac{4}{5}$

11. 0.25 $>$ $\frac{1}{7}$ 12. 1.8 $>$ $\frac{12}{7}$

13. 0.625 $>$ $\frac{4}{8}$ 14. 0.33 $=$ $\frac{1}{3}$

15. Jenna looked carefully at the labels on two different types of cookies. The chocolate ones had $\frac{3}{4}$ pound in the package. The package of vanilla cookies claimed it had 0.67 pound of cookies inside. Were the chocolate cookies <, > or = to the vanilla cookies? $\frac{3}{4} > 0.67$

45

Mixed Numbers and Improper Fractions

A **mixed number** is a whole number and a fraction, such as $1\frac{1}{3}$. An **improper fraction** has a numerator that is larger than its denominator, such as $\frac{9}{7}$. To write an improper fraction as a mixed number, divide the numerator by the denominator. The quotient becomes the whole number and the remainder becomes the fraction.

Examples:

$\frac{16}{3} = 3\overline{)16} = 5\frac{1}{3}$ $\frac{28}{5} = 5\overline{)28} = 5\frac{3}{5}$

To change a mixed number into an improper fraction, multiply the whole number by the denominator and add the numerator.

Examples:

$4\frac{1}{3} = 4 \times 3 = 12 + 1 = 13 \quad \frac{13}{3}$

$8\frac{4}{7} = 8 \times 7 = 56 + 4 = 60 \quad \frac{60}{7}$

Directions: Follow the instructions below.

1. Change the improper fractions to mixed numbers and reduce to lowest terms. Use another sheet of paper if necessary. The first one has been done for you.

a. $\frac{34}{6} = 6\overline{)34} = 5\frac{4}{6} = 5\frac{2}{3}$

b. $\frac{65}{4} = 16\frac{1}{4}$ c. $\frac{23}{8} = 2\frac{7}{8}$ d. $\frac{89}{3} = 29\frac{2}{3}$

e. $\frac{45}{9} = 5$ f. $\frac{32}{5} = 6\frac{2}{5}$ g. $\frac{13}{7} = 1\frac{6}{7}$

h. $\frac{24}{9} = 2\frac{2}{3}$ i. $\frac{31}{2} = 15\frac{1}{2}$ j. $\frac{84}{23} = 3\frac{15}{23}$

2. Change these mixed numbers into improper fractions. The first one has been done for you.

a. $4\frac{6}{7} = 4 \times 7 = 28 + 6 = \frac{34}{7}$ b. $2\frac{1}{9} = \frac{19}{9}$ c. $5\frac{4}{5} = \frac{29}{5}$ d. $12\frac{1}{4} = \frac{49}{4}$

e. $6\frac{7}{8} = \frac{55}{8}$ f. $3\frac{9}{11} = \frac{42}{11}$ g. $8\frac{3}{12} = \frac{99}{12}$ h. $1\frac{6}{14} = \frac{20}{14}$ i. $4\frac{2}{3} = \frac{14}{3}$ j. $9\frac{4}{15} = \frac{139}{15}$

46

Review

Directions: Match the following mixed numbers with the equivalent improper fractions.

1. $\frac{25}{4}$ = ___D___   A. $13\frac{2}{5}$

2. $\frac{32}{6}$ = ___G___   B. $9\frac{1}{2}$

3. $\frac{17}{2}$ = _C or H_   C. $8\frac{1}{2}$

4. $\frac{84}{9}$ = ___M___   D. $6\frac{1}{4}$

5. $\frac{65}{5}$ = ___A___   E. $26\frac{2}{3}$

6. $\frac{94}{6}$ = ___L___   F. $9\frac{2}{7}$

7. $\frac{48}{5}$ = ___K___   G. $5\frac{1}{3}$

8. $\frac{99}{12}$ = ___J___   H. $0.8\frac{1}{2}$

9. $\frac{57}{6}$ = ___B___   I. $16\frac{2}{3}$

10. $\frac{65}{7}$ = ___F___   J. $8\frac{1}{4}$

11. $\frac{87}{15}$ = ___N___   K. $9\frac{3}{5}$

12. $\frac{34}{6}$ = _H or C_   L. $11\frac{3}{4}$

13. $\frac{53}{2}$ = ___E___   M. $9\frac{1}{3}$

14. $\frac{82}{6}$ = ___I___   N. $5\frac{4}{5}$

15. $\frac{78}{9}$ = ___O___   O. $8\frac{2}{3}$

47

Adding Fractions

When adding fractions, if the denominators are the same, simply add the numerators. When the result is an improper fraction, change it to a mixed number.

Examples: $\frac{3}{5} + \frac{1}{5} = \frac{4}{5}$ $\frac{3}{9} + \frac{7}{9} = \frac{10}{9} = 1\frac{1}{9}$

If the denominators of fractions are different, change them so they are the same. To do this, find equivalent fractions. In the first example below, $\frac{1}{4}$ and $\frac{1}{8}$ have different denominators, so change $\frac{1}{4}$ to the equivalent fraction $\frac{2}{8}$. Then add the numerators. In the second example, $\frac{2}{7}$ and $\frac{1}{3}$ also have different denominators. Find a denominator both 7 and 3 divide into. The lowest number they both divide into is 21. Multiply the numerator and denominator of $\frac{2}{7}$ by 3 to get the equivalent fraction $\frac{6}{21}$. Then multiply the numerator and denominator of $\frac{1}{3}$ by 7 to get the equivalent fraction $\frac{7}{21}$.

Examples:

Directions: Solve the following problems. Find equivalent fractions when necessary.

1. $\frac{3}{5}$ + $\frac{1}{5}$ = $\frac{4}{5}$

2. $\frac{7}{8}$ + $\frac{9}{16}$ = $\frac{16}{16} = 1$

3. $\frac{1}{9}$ + $\frac{2}{3}$ = $\frac{6}{9} = \frac{2}{3}$

4. $\frac{2}{3}$ + $\frac{1}{5}$ = $\frac{13}{15}$

5. $\frac{2}{15}$ + $\frac{1}{5}$ = $\frac{5}{15} = \frac{1}{3}$

6. Cora is making a cake. She needs $\frac{1}{2}$ cup butter for the cake and $\frac{1}{4}$ cup butter for the frosting. How much butter does she need altogether? $\frac{3}{4}$

7. Henry is painting a wall. Yesterday he painted $\frac{1}{3}$ of it. Today he painted $\frac{1}{4}$ of it. How much has he painted altogether? $\frac{7}{12}$

8. Nancy ate $\frac{1}{6}$ of a pie. Her father ate $\frac{1}{4}$ of it. How much did they eat altogether? $\frac{5}{12}$

48

Subtracting Fractions

Subtracting fractions is very similar to adding them in that the denominators must be the same. If the denominators are different, use equivalent fractions.

Examples:

Adding and subtracting mixed numbers are also similar. Often, though, change the mixed numbers to improper fractions. If the denominators are different, use equivalent fractions.

Examples:

Directions: Solve the following problems. Use equivalent fractions and improper fractions where necessary.

1. $\frac{6}{7}$ − $\frac{5}{7}$ = $\frac{1}{7}$

2. $\frac{2}{9}$ − $\frac{4}{9}$ = $\frac{7}{9}$

3. $2\frac{3}{6}$ − $\frac{2}{6}$ = $5\frac{1}{30} = 1\frac{7}{10}$

4. $\frac{3}{4}$ − $\frac{1}{2}$ = $\frac{1}{4}$

5. $2\frac{1}{3}$ − $\frac{2}{3}$ = $\frac{19}{14} = 1\frac{7}{12}$

6. Carol promised to weed the flower garden for $1\frac{1}{2}$ hours this morning. So far she has pulled two weeds for $\frac{3}{4}$ of an hour. How much longer does she have to work? $\frac{3}{4}$ hour

7. Dil started out with $1\frac{1}{2}$ gallons of paint. He used $\frac{7}{8}$ of the paint on his boat. How much paint is left? $\frac{7}{8}$ gallon

8. A certain movie lasts $2\frac{1}{2}$ hours. Susan has already watched it for $1\frac{2}{3}$ hours. How much longer is the movie? $\frac{5}{6}$ hour

9. Bert didn't finish $\frac{1}{8}$ of the math problems on a test. He made mistakes on $\frac{1}{6}$ of the problems. The rest he answered correctly. What fraction of the problems did he answer correctly? $\frac{17}{24}$ problems

49

Multiplying Fractions

To multiply two fractions, multiply the numerators and then multiply the denominators. If necessary, change the answer to its lowest term.

Examples: $\frac{3}{4} \times \frac{2}{6} = \frac{6}{12} = \frac{1}{2}$ $\frac{1}{8} \times \frac{4}{5} = \frac{4}{40} = \frac{1}{10}$

To multiply a whole number by a fraction, first write the whole number as a fraction (with 1 as the denominator). Then multiply as above. You may need to change an improper fraction to a mixed number.

Examples: $\frac{2}{3} \times \frac{4}{1} = \frac{8}{3} = 2\frac{2}{3}$ $\frac{3}{7} \times \frac{6}{1} = \frac{18}{7} = 2\frac{4}{7}$

Directions: Solve the following problems, writing answers in their lowest terms.

1. $\frac{1}{5} \times \frac{2}{3} = \frac{2}{15}$ 2. $\frac{1}{3} \times \frac{4}{7} = \frac{4}{21}$ 3. $\frac{2}{8} \times 3 = \frac{6}{8} = 3\frac{3}{4}$ 4. $\frac{2}{5} \times \frac{1}{2} = \frac{2}{15} = \frac{1}{6}$

5. Tim lost $\frac{1}{8}$ of his marbles. If he had 56 marbles, how many did he lose? 7 marbles

6. Jeff is making $\frac{5}{6}$ of a recipe for spaghetti sauce. How much will he need of each ingredient below?

$1\frac{1}{2}$ cups water = ___5/6 cup___ 2 cups tomato paste = ___$1\frac{1}{3}$ cups___

$\frac{3}{4}$ teaspoon oregano = ___1/2 tsp.___ $4\frac{1}{2}$ teaspoons salt = ___3 tsp.___

7. Carrie bought 2 dozen donuts and asked for $\frac{3}{4}$ of them to be chocolate. How many were chocolate? ___18___

8. Christy let her hair grow 14 inches long and then had $\frac{1}{4}$ of it cut off. How much was cut off? ___$3\frac{1}{2}$ in.___

9. Kurt has finished $\frac{7}{8}$ of 40 math problems. How many has he done? ___35___

10. If Sherryl's cat eats $\frac{2}{3}$ can of cat food every day, how many cans should Sherryl buy for a week? ___$4\frac{2}{3}$___

50

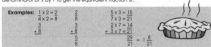
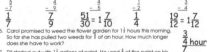
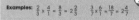

Dividing Fractions

Reciprocals are two fractions that, when multiplied together, make 1. To divide a fraction by a fraction, turn one of the fractions upside down and multiply. The upside-down fraction is a reciprocal of its original fraction. If you multiply a fraction by its reciprocal, you always get 1.

Examples of reciprocals: $\frac{2}{3} \times \frac{3}{2} = \frac{6}{6} = 1$ $\frac{9}{11} \times \frac{11}{9} = \frac{99}{99} = 1$

Examples of dividing by fractions: $\frac{1}{2} \div \frac{2}{3} = \frac{1}{2} \times \frac{3}{2} = \frac{3}{4}$ $\frac{2}{5} \div \frac{2}{7} = \frac{2}{5} \times \frac{7}{2} = \frac{14}{10} = \frac{7}{5} = 1\frac{2}{5}$

To divide a whole number by a fraction, first write the whole number as a fraction (with a denominator of 1). (Write a mixed number as an improper fraction.) Then finish the problem as explained above.

Examples: $4 \div \frac{2}{6} = \frac{4}{1} \times \frac{6}{2} = \frac{24}{2} = 12$ $3\frac{1}{2} \div \frac{2}{7} = \frac{7}{2} \times \frac{7}{2} = \frac{35}{4} = 8\frac{3}{4}$

Directions: Solve the following problems, writing answers in their lowest terms. Change any improper fractions to mixed numbers.

1. $\frac{1}{3} \div \frac{2}{5} = \frac{5}{6}$ 2. $\frac{6}{7} \div \frac{1}{3} = \frac{18}{7} = 2\frac{4}{7}$ 3. $3 \div \frac{3}{4} = \frac{12}{3} = 4$ 4. $\frac{1}{2} \div \frac{2}{3} = \frac{3}{8}$

5. Judy has 8 candy bars. She wants to give $\frac{1}{3}$ of a candy bar to everyone in her class. Does she have enough for all 24 students?   Yes

6. A big jar of glue holds $3\frac{1}{2}$ cups. How many little containers that hold $\frac{1}{4}$ cup each can you fill?   14 containers

7. A container holds 27 ounces of ice cream. How many $4\frac{1}{2}$-ounce servings is that?   6 servings

8. It takes $2\frac{1}{2}$ teaspoons of powdered mix to make 1 cup of hot chocolate. How many cups can you make with 45 teaspoons of mix?   18 cups

9. Each cup of hot chocolate also takes $\frac{2}{3}$ cup of milk. How many cups of hot chocolate can you make with 12 cups of milk?   18 cups

51

Review

Directions: Follow the instructions below.

1. Write each of these decimals as fractions
   a. $0.43 = \frac{43}{100}$ b. $0.6 = \frac{6}{10}$ c. $0.783 = \frac{783}{1,000}$ d. $0.91 = \frac{91}{100}$

2. Write each of these fractions as decimals, rounding them off to the nearest hundredth
   a. $\frac{3}{10} = 0.3$ b. $\frac{4}{7} = 0.57$ c. $\frac{3}{9} = 0.33$ d. $\frac{64}{100} = 0.64$

3. Write two equivalent fractions for each of these
   a. $\frac{2}{3} = \frac{4}{6}, \frac{8}{12}$ b. $\frac{1}{4} = \frac{2}{8}, \frac{3}{12}$ c. $\frac{5}{8} = \frac{10}{16}, \frac{15}{24}$

4. Change these fractions into their lowest terms
   a. $\frac{4}{16} = \frac{1}{4}$ b. $\frac{6}{18} = \frac{1}{3}$ c. $\frac{5}{90} = \frac{1}{18}$ d. $\frac{9}{24} = \frac{3}{8}$

5. Change these improper fractions into mixed numbers
   a. $\frac{30}{9} = 3\frac{1}{3}$ b. $\frac{46}{3} = 15\frac{1}{3}$ c. $\frac{38}{6} = 6\frac{1}{3}$ d. $\frac{18}{4} = 4\frac{1}{2}$

6. Change these mixed numbers into improper fractions
   a. $3\frac{1}{6} = \frac{19}{6}$ b. $7\frac{1}{7} = \frac{50}{7}$ c. $4\frac{2}{7} = \frac{30}{7}$ d. $8\frac{1}{9} = \frac{73}{9}$

7. George has written $1\frac{1}{4}$ pages of a report that is supposed to be $3\frac{1}{2}$ pages long. How much more does he have to write? $2\frac{3}{4}$

8. Jackie ate $\frac{3}{8}$ of half a cake. How much of the whole cake did she eat? $\frac{3}{16}$

9. Connie's family is driving to Los Angeles. They drove $\frac{1}{6}$ of the way the first day and $\frac{1}{5}$ of the way the second day. How much of the trip have they completed so far? $\frac{11}{30}$

10. Kenny gets $6 a week for his allowance. He saved $\frac{1}{3}$ of it last week and $\frac{1}{2}$ of it this week. How much money did he save in these 2 weeks? $5

11. Of 32 students in one class, $\frac{3}{8}$ have a brother or sister. How many students are only children?   12

12. In one class, $\frac{1}{5}$ of the students were born in January, $\frac{1}{10}$ in February and $\frac{1}{10}$ in March. How much of the class was born in these 3 months? $\frac{2}{5}$

52

Review

Directions: Follow the instructions below.

Add.

1. $\frac{4}{16} + \frac{5}{8} = \frac{14}{16} = \frac{7}{8}$ 2. $\frac{1}{6} + \frac{1}{3} = \frac{3}{6} = \frac{1}{2}$ 3. $\frac{2}{10} + \frac{4}{5} = \frac{10}{10} = 1$ 4. $\frac{3}{5} + \frac{9}{10} = \frac{15}{10} = \frac{3}{2} = 1\frac{1}{2}$

Subtract.

1. $\frac{15}{16} - \frac{2}{8} = \frac{9}{16} = 1$ 2. $\frac{3}{9} - \frac{3}{9} = \frac{3}{8}$ 3. $\frac{4}{8} - \frac{2}{14} = \frac{6}{7} = \frac{3}{8}$ 4. $\frac{3}{7} - \frac{1}{14} = \frac{5}{10} = \frac{1}{2} \, \frac{}{10}$

Multiply.

1. $\frac{1}{2} \times \frac{4}{16} = \frac{4}{32} = \frac{1}{8}$ 2. $\frac{1}{3} \times \frac{4}{9} = \frac{4}{27}$ 3. $\frac{5}{12} \times \frac{1}{4} = \frac{5}{48}$ 4. $\frac{3}{16} \times \frac{3}{4} = \frac{9}{64}$

Divide.

1. $\frac{3}{5} \div \frac{1}{3} = \frac{9}{5} = 1\frac{4}{5}$ 2. $4 \div \frac{1}{2} = \frac{8}{1} = 8$ 3. $\frac{1}{4} \div \frac{1}{3} = \frac{3}{4}$ 4. $3\frac{1}{3} \div \frac{1}{3} = \frac{45}{4} = 11\frac{1}{4}$

Write >, < or = to make the statements true.

1. $0.5 \; < \; \frac{5}{8}$ 2. $0.8 \; = \; \frac{4}{5}$ 3. $0.35 \; < \; \frac{2}{5}$ 4. $1.3 \; > \; \frac{7}{8}$

53

Perimeter

The **perimeter** is the distance around a shape formed by straight lines, such as a square or triangle. To find the perimeter of a shape, add the lengths of its sides.

Examples:

For the square, add $8 + 8 + 8 + 8 = 32$. Or, write a formula using **P** for **perimeter** and **s** for the **sides**: $P = 4 \times s$
$P = 4 \times 8$
$P = 32$ inches

For the rectangle, add $4 + 5 + 4 + 5 = 18$. Or, use a different formula, using **l** for **length** and **w** for **width**. In formulas with parentheses, first do the adding, multiplying, and so on, in the parentheses.: $P = (2 \times l) + (2 \times w)$
$P = (2 \times 5) + (2 \times 4)$
$P = 10 + 8$
$P = 18$

For the triangle, the sides are all different lengths, so the formula doesn't help. Instead, add the sides: $3 + 4 + 5 = 12$ inches.

Directions: Find the perimeter of each shape below. Use the formula whenever possible.

1. Find the perimeter of the room pictured at left.   P = 42 ft.

2. Brandy plans to frame a picture with a sheet of construction paper. Her picture is 8 in. wide and 13 in. long. She wants the frame to extend 1 in. beyond the picture on all sides. How wide and long should the frame be? What is the perimeter of her picture and of the frame?
   Length and width of frame: 15 in. long, 10 in. wide
   Perimeter of picture: 42 in.
   Perimeter of frame: 50 in.

3. A square has a perimeter of 120 feet. How long is each side?   30 ft.

4. A triangle with equal sides has a perimeter of 96 inches. How long is each side?   32 in.

5. A rectangle has two sides that are each 14 feet long and a perimeter of 50 feet. How wide is it?   11 ft.

54

Perimeter

Directions: Find the perimeter of each shape below.

1. P = 12
2. P = 32
3. P = 128
4. P = 18
5. P = 16
6. P = 14
7. P = 25
8. P = 21

55

Area: Squares and Rectangles

The **area** is the number of square units that covers a certain space. To find the area, multiply the length by the width. The answer is in square units, shown by adding a superscript 2 (^{2}) to the number.

Examples:

For the rectangle, use this formula: **A = l x w**
$A = 8 \times 5$
$A = 40$ in.^{2}

For the square formula, **s** stands for side: **A = s x s** (or s^2)
$A = 3 \times 3$ (or 3^2)
$A = 9$ in.^{2}

Directions: Find the area of each shape below.

1. Find the area of a room which is 12 feet long and 7 feet wide.   A = 84 ft.^{2}

2. A farmer's field is 32 feet on each side. How many square feet does he have to plow?   1,024 ft.^{2}

3. Steve's bedroom is 10 feet by 12 feet. How many square feet of carpeting would cover the floor?   120 ft.^{2}

4. Two of Steve's walls are 7.5 feet high and 12 feet long. The other two are the same height and 10 feet long. How many square feet of wallpaper would cover all four walls?
   Square feet for 12-foot wall = 90 ft.^{2} x 2 = 180 ft.^{2}
   Square feet for 10-foot wall = 75 ft.^{2} x 2 = 150 ft.^{2}

5. A clothes shop moved from a store that was 35 by 22 feet to a new location that was 53 by 32 feet. How many more square feet does the store have now?
   Square feet for first location = 770 ft.^{2}
   Square feet for new location = 1,696 ft.^{2} Difference = 926 ft.^{2}

6. A school wanted to purchase a climber for the playground. The one they selected would need 98 square feet of space. The only space available on the playground was 12 feet long and 8 feet wide. Will there be enough space for the climber?   No

56

Area: Triangles

Finding the area of a triangle requires knowing the size of the base and the height. For the triangle formula, use **b** for **base** and **h** for **height**. Multiply ½ times the size of the base and then multiply by the height. The answer will be in square units.

Example:

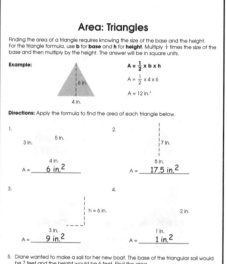

$A = \frac{1}{2} \times b \times h$

$A = \frac{1}{2} \times 4 \times 6$

$A = 12$ in.²

Directions: Apply the formula to find the area of each triangle below.

1. 3 in.   5 in.
    4 in.
    A = __6 in.²__

2. 7 in.
    5 in.
    A = __17.5 in.²__

3. h = 6 in.
    3 in.
    A = __9 in.²__

4. 2 in.
    1 in.
    A = __1 in.²__

5. Diane wanted to make a sail for her new boat. The base of the triangular sail would be 7 feet and the height would be 6 feet. Find the area.

A = __21 ft.²__

57

Circles

The **circumference** is the distance around a circle. The **diameter** is the length of a line that divides the circle in half. The **radius** is the length of a line from the center of the circle to the outside edge. The formulas used to find the circumference and area of a circle include the Greek letter π (pronounced "pie"), which equals 3.14. To find the circumference (**C**) of a circle when you know the diameter (**d**), use this formula: **C = π x d**. To find the circumference when you know the radius (**r**), use this formula: **C = π x (r + r)**. To find the area (**A**) of a circle, use this formula: **A = π x r x r**.

Examples:

C = π x d   C = π x (r + r)   A = π x r x r
C = 3.14 x 15   C = 3.14 x (3 + 3)   A = 3.14 x 3 x 3
C = 47.1 inches   C = 18.84 inches   A = 28.26 in.²

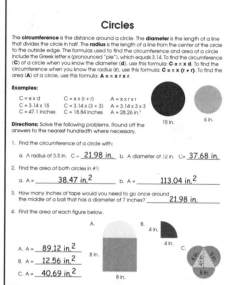

15 in.   6 in.

Directions: Solve the following problems. Round off the answers to the nearest hundredth where necessary.

1. Find the circumference of a circle with:

   a. radius of 3.5 in. C = __21.98 in.__   b. a diameter of 12 in. C = __37.68 in.__

2. Find the area of both circles in #1:

   a. A = __38.47 in.²__   b. A = __113.04 in.²__

3. How many inches of tape would you need to go once around the middle of a ball that has a diameter of 7 inches? __21.98 in.__

4. Find the area of each figure below.

   A.   B. 4 in.   C.
               4 in.
   8 in.

   8 in.

   A. A = __89.12 in.²__
   B. A = __12.56 in.²__
   C. A = __40.69 in.²__

58

Volume

Volume is the number of cubic units that fills a space. A **cubic unit** has 6 equal sides, like a child's block. To find the volume (**V**) of something, multiply the length (**l**) by the width (**w**) by the height (**h**), or **V = l x w x h**. The answer will be in cubic units (³). Sometimes it's easier to understand volume if you imagine a figure is made of small cubes.

Example: V = l x w x h
            V = 4 x 6 x 5
            V = 120 in.³

Directions: Solve the following problems.

1. What is the volume of a cube that is 7 inches on each side? __343 in.³__

2. How many cubic inches of cereal are in a box that is 10 inches long, 6 inches wide and 4.5 inches high? __270 in.³__

3. Jeremy made a tower of five blocks that are each 2.5 inches square. How many cubic inches are in his tower? __78.125 in.³__

4. How many cubic feet of gravel are in the back of a full dump truck that measures 7 feet wide by 4 feet tall by 16 feet long? __448 in.³__

5. Will 1,000 cubic inches of dirt fill a flower box that is 32 inches long, 7 inches wide and 7 inches tall? __Yes__

6. A mouse needs 100 cubic inches of air to live for an hour. Will your pet mouse be okay for an hour in an airtight box that's 4.5 inches wide by 8.25 inches long by 2.5 inches high? __No__

7. Find the volume of the figures below. 1 cube = 1 inch³

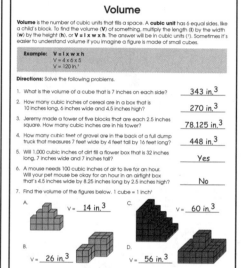

A.   V = __14 in.³__   C.   V = __60 in.³__
B.   V = __26 in.³__   D.   V = __56 in.³__

59

Area Challenge

When finding the area of an unusual shape, first try to divide it into squares, rectangles or triangles. Find the area of each of those parts, then add your answers together to find the total area of the object.

Directions: Find the area of each shape below.

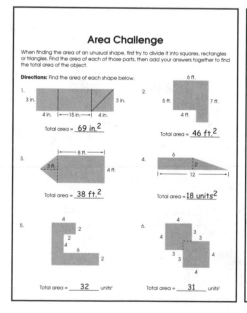

1. 3 in.   3 in.
    4 in. — 15 in. — 4 in.
    Total area = __69 in.²__

2. 6 ft.
    5 ft.   7 ft.
    4 ft.
    Total area = __46 ft.²__

3. 8 ft.
    3 ft.   4 ft.
    12
    Total area = __38 ft.²__

4. 6
    2
    Total area = __18 units²__

5. 4
    2
    2
    4
    6
    2
    Total area = __32__ units²

6. 4
    4   3
        3
    3   4
        4
    Total area = __31__ units²

60

Lines

The following terms and definitions are used in geometry and represented by symbols.

Term	Definition	Symbol
Angle:	The amount of space where two lines meet	
Line:	A series of continuous points in a straight path, extending in either direction	
Line Segment:	A straight line extending from one exact point to another	
Intersecting Lines:	At least two straight lines that cross each other's paths	
Parallel Lines:	Lines that never get closer together or farther apart at any point	
Perpendicular Lines:	Two lines that intersect each other at a 90° angle	
Ray:	A straight line extending in one direction from one specific point	
Vertex:	The point at which two lines intersect	

Directions: Study the diagram and fill in the corresponding letters and symbols that represent the following:

Answers will vary. Sample answers:

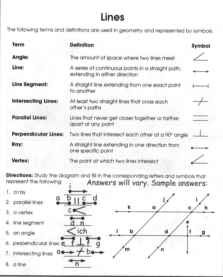

1. a ray
2. parallel lines
3. a vertex
4. line segment
5. an angle
6. perpendicular lines
7. intersecting lines
8. a line

61

Angles

Angles are named according to the number of degrees between the lines. The degrees are measured with a protractor.

Examples:

straight angle   right angle   acute angle   obtuse angle
(measures 180°)   (90°)   (less than 90°)   (more than 90°)

Directions: Study the examples. Then follow the instructions below.

1. Use a protractor to measure each angle below. Then write whether it is straight, right, acute or obtuse.

   A.   Degrees: __60°__   C.   Degrees: __120°__
        Kind of angle: __acute__   Kind of angle: __obtuse__

   B.   Degrees: __180°__   D.   Degrees: __90°__
        Kind of angle: __straight__   Kind of angle: __right__

2. The angles in this figure are named by letters. Write the number of degrees in each angle and whether it is straight, right, acute or obtuse.

   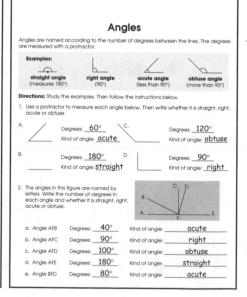

   a. Angle AFB   Degrees: __40°__   Kind of angle: __acute__
   b. Angle AFC   Degrees: __90°__   Kind of angle: __right__
   c. Angle AFD   Degrees: __100°__   Kind of angle: __obtuse__
   d. Angle AFE   Degrees: __180°__   Kind of angle: __straight__
   e. Angle BFD   Degrees: __80°__   Kind of angle: __acute__

62

Types of Triangles

The sum of angles in all triangles is 180°. However, triangles come in different shapes. They are categorized by the length of their sides and by their types of angles.

Equilateral: Three equal sides

Acute: Three acute angles

Isosceles: Two equal sides

Right: One right angle

Scalene: Zero equal sides

Obtuse: One obtuse angle

One triangle can be a combination of types, such as isosceles and obtuse.

Directions: Study the examples. Then complete the exercises below.

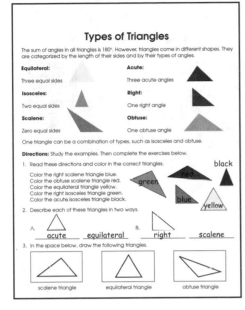

1. Read these directions and color in the correct triangles.

Color the right scalene triangle blue.
Color the obtuse scalene triangle red.
Color the equilateral triangle yellow.
Color the right isosceles triangle green.
Color the acute isosceles triangle black.

2. Describe each of these triangles in two ways.

A. __acute__ __equilateral__   B. __right__ __scalene__

3. In the space below, draw the following triangles.

scalene triangle   equilateral triangle   obtuse triangle

63

Finding Angles

All triangles have three angles. The sum of these angles is 180°. Therefore, if we know the number of degrees in two of the angles, we can add them together, then subtract from 180 to find the size of the third angle.

Directions: Follow the instructions below.

1. Circle the number that shows the third angle of triangles A through F. Then describe each triangle two ways. The first one has been done for you.

A. 60°, 60°	45° 50° (60°)	equilateral, acute
B. 35°, 55°	27° (90°) 132°	scalene, right
C. 30°, 120°	(30°) 74° 112°	isosceles, obtuse
D. 15°, 78°	65° (87°) 98°	scalene, acute
E. 28°, 93°	61° (59°) 70°	scalene, obtuse
F. 12°, 114°	60° 50° (54°)	scalene, obtuse

2. Find the number of degrees in the third angle of each triangle below.

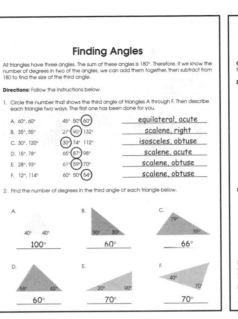

A. 40° 40° __100°__

B. 90° 30° __60°__

C. 79° 35° __66°__

D. 58° 62° __60°__

E. 20° 90° __70°__

F. 40° 70° __70°__

64

Geometry Gems

Geometry is the study of lines and angles, the shapes they create and how they relate to one another.

Directions: Match the following shapes with their names.

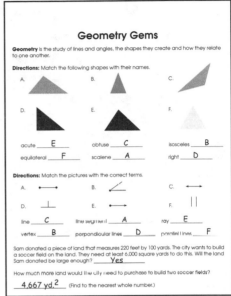

A.   B.   C.   D.   E.   F.

acute __E__   obtuse __C__   isosceles __B__

equilateral __F__   scalene __A__   right __D__

Directions: Match the pictures with the correct terms.

A.   B.   C.   D.   E.   F.

line __C__   line segment __A__   ray __E__

vertex __B__   perpendicular lines __D__   parallel lines __F__

Sam donated a piece of land that measures 220 feet by 100 yards. The city wants to build a soccer field on the land. They need at least 6,000 square yards to do this. Will the land Sam donated be large enough? __Yes__

How much more land would the city need to purchase to build two soccer fields?

__4,667 yd.²__   (Find to the nearest whole number.)

65

Geometric Patterns

Geometric patterns can be described in several ways. **Similar shapes** have the same shape but in differing sizes. **Congruent shapes** have the same geometric pattern but may be facing in different directions. **Symmetrical shapes** are identical when divided in half.

Directions: Use the terms **similar**, **congruent** or **symmetrical** to describe the following patterns.

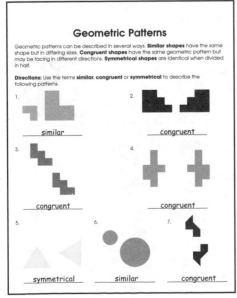

1. similar   2. congruent

3. congruent   4. congruent

5. symmetrical   6. similar   7. congruent

66

Types of Quadrilaterals

A **quadrilateral** is a shape with four sides and four angles. The sum of angles in all quadrilaterals is 360°. Like triangles, quadrilaterals come in different shapes and are categorized by their sides and their angles.

A **square** has four parallel sides of equal length and four 90° angles.

A **rectangle** has four parallel sides, but only its opposite sides are equal length; it has four 90° angles.

A **parallelogram** has four parallel sides, with the opposite sides of equal length, but all its angles are more or less than 90°.

A **trapezoid** has two opposite sides that are parallel; its sides may or may not be equal length; its angles may include none, one or two that are 90°.

Directions: Study the examples. Then complete the exercises below.

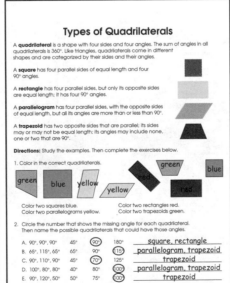

1. Color in the correct quadrilaterals.

green   blue   yellow   red   green   blue   yellow   red

Color two squares blue.   Color two rectangles red.
Color two parallelograms yellow.   Color two trapezoids green.

2. Circle the number that shows the missing angle for each quadrilateral. Then name the possible quadrilaterals that could have those angles.

A. 90°, 90°, 90°	45°	(90°)	180°	square, rectangle
B. 65°, 115°, 65°	65°	90°	(115°)	parallelogram, trapezoid
C. 90°, 110°, 90°	45°	(70°)	125°	trapezoid
D. 100°, 80°, 80°	40°	80°	(100°)	parallelogram, trapezoid
E. 90°, 120°, 50°	50°	75°	(100°)	trapezoid

67

Review

Directions: Complete the following exercises.

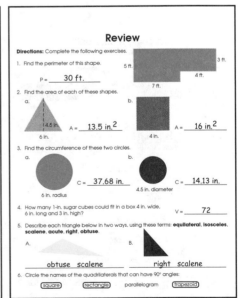

1. Find the perimeter of this shape.   5 ft.   3 ft.   4 ft.   7 ft.

P = __30 ft.__

2. Find the area of each of these shapes.

a. 6 in. 4.5 in.   A = __13.5 in.²__

b. 4 in.   A = __16 in.²__

3. Find the circumference of these two circles.

a. 6 in. radius   C = __37.68 in.__

b. 4.5 in. diameter   C = __14.13 in.__

4. How many 1-in. sugar cubes could fit in a box 4 in. wide, 6 in. long and 3 in. high?   V = __72__

5. Describe each triangle below in two ways, using these terms: **equilateral**, **isosceles**, **scalene**, **acute**, **right**, **obtuse**.

A. __obtuse__ __scalene__   B. __right__ __scalene__

6. Circle the names of the quadrilaterals that can have 90° angles:

(square) (rectangle) parallelogram (trapezoid)

68

Length in Customary Units

The **customary system** of measurement is the most widely used in the United States. It measures length in inches, feet, yards and miles.

Examples:

12 inches (in.) = 1 foot (ft.)
3 ft. (36 in.) = 1 yard (yd.)
5,280 ft. (1,760 yds.) = 1 mile (mi.)

To change to a larger unit, divide. To change to a smaller unit, multiply.

Examples:

To change inches to feet, divide by 12.	24 in. = 2 ft.
To change feet to inches, multiply by 12.	3 ft. = 36 in.
To change feet to yards, divide by 36.	108 in. = 3 yd.
To change yards to feet, multiply by 3.	12 ft. = 4 yd.
	27 in. = 2 ft. 3 in.
	4 ft. = 48 in.
	80 in. = 2 yd. 8 in.
	11 ft. = 3 yd. 2 ft.

Sometimes in subtraction you have to borrow units.

Examples:
```
  3 ft. 4 in. = 2 ft. 16 in.        3 yd.     = 2 yd. 3 ft.
- 1 ft. 11 in. = 1 ft. 11 in.     - 1 yd. 2 ft. - 1 yd. 2 ft.
               1 ft. 5 in.                     1 yd. 1 ft.
```

Directions: Solve the following problems.

1. 108 in. = _9_ ft.
2. 68 in. = _12_ ft. _8_ in.
3. _3_ yd. _2_ ft.
4. 3,520 yd. = _2_ mi.

5. What form of measurement (inches, feet, yards or miles) would you use for each item below?

a. pencil _inches_   b. vacation trip _miles_
c. playground _yards or feet_   d. wall _feet or yards_

6. One side of a square box is 2 ft. 4 in. What is the perimeter of the box? _9 ft. 6 in._
7. Jason is 59 in. tall. Kent is 5 ft. 1 in. tall. Who is taller and by how much? _Kent, 2 in._
8. Karen bought a doll 2 ft. 8 in. tall for her little sister. She found a box that is 29 in. long. Will the doll fit in that box? _No_
9. Dan's dog likes to go out in the backyard, which is 85 ft. wide. The dog's chain is 17 ft. 6 in. long. If Dan attaches one end of the chain to a pole in the middle of the yard, will his dog be able to leave the yard? _No_

69

Length in Metric Units

The **metric system** measures length in meters, centimeters, millimeters, and kilometers.

Examples:

A **meter (m)** is about 40 inches or 3.3 feet.
A **centimeter (cm)** is 1/100 of a meter or 0.4 inches.
A **millimeter (mm)** is 1/1000 of a meter or 0.04 inches.
A **kilometer (km)** is 1,000 meters or 0.6 miles.

As before, divide to find a larger unit and multiply to find a smaller unit.

Examples:
```
To change cm to mm, multiply by 10.
To change cm to meters, divide by 100.
To change mm to meters, divide by 1,000.
To change km to meters, multiply by 1,000.
```
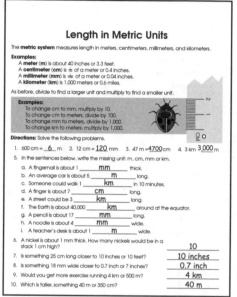

Directions: Solve the following problems.

1. 600 cm = _6_ m
2. 12 cm = _120_ mm
3. 47 m = _4700_ cm
4. 3 km _3,000_ m

5. In the sentences below, write the missing unit: m, cm, mm or km.

a. A fingernail is about 1 _mm_ thick.
b. An average car is about 5 _m_ long.
c. Someone could walk 1 _km_ in 10 minutes.
d. A finger is about 7 _cm_ long.
e. A street could be 3 _km_ long.
f. The Earth is about 40,000 _km_ around at the equator.
g. A pencil is about 17 _mm_ long.
h. A noodle is about 4 _mm_ wide.
i. A teacher's desk is about 1 _m_ wide.

6. A nickel is about 1 mm thick. How many nickels would be in a stack 1 cm high? _10_
7. Is something 25 cm long closer to 10 inches or 10 feet? _10 inches_
8. Is something 18 mm wide closer to 0.7 inch or 7 inches? _0.7 inch_
9. Would you get more exercise running 4 km or 500 m? _4 km_
10. Which is taller, something 40 m or 350 cm? _40 m_

70

Weight in Customary Units

Here are the main ways to measure weight in customary units:

16 ounces (oz.) = 1 pound (lb.)
2,000 lb. = 1 ton (tn.)

To change ounces to pounds, divide by 16.
To change pounds to ounces, multiply by 16.

As with measurements of length, you may have to borrow units in subtraction.

Example:
```
  4 lb. 5 oz. = 3 lb. 21 oz.
- 2 lb. 10 oz. - 2 lb. 10 oz.
              1 lb. 11 oz.
```

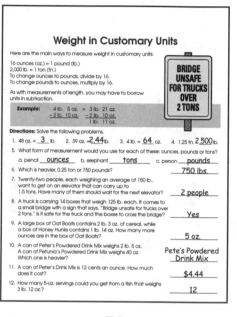

Directions: Solve the following problems.

1. 48 oz. = _3_ lb.
2. 39 oz. = _2.44_ lb.
3. 4 lb. = _64_ oz.
4. 1.25 oz _2,500_ lb.

5. What form of measurement would you use for each of these: ounces, pounds or tons?

a. pencil _ounces_   b. elephant _tons_   c. person _pounds_

6. Which is heavier, 0.25 ton or 750 pounds? _750 lbs_
7. Twenty-two people, each weighing an average of 150 lb., want to get on an elevator that can carry up to 1.5 tons. How many of them should wait for the next elevator? _2 people_
8. A truck is carrying 14 boxes that weigh 125 lb. each. It comes to a small bridge with a sign that says, "Bridge unsafe for trucks over 2 tons." Is it safe for the truck and the boxes to cross the bridge? _Yes_
9. A large box of Oat Boats contains 2 lb. 3 oz. of cereal, while a box of Honey Hunks contains 1 lb. 14 oz. How many more ounces are in the box of Oat Boats? _5 oz._
10. A can of Peter's Powdered Drink Mix weighs 2 lb. 5 oz. A can of Petunia's Powdered Drink Mix weighs 40 oz. Which one is heavier? _Pete's Powdered Drink Mix_
11. A can of Peter's Drink Mix is 12 cents an ounce. How much does it cost? _$4.44_
12. How many 5-oz. servings could you get from a fish that weighs 3 lb. 12 oz.? _12_

71

Weight in Metric Units

A **gram (g)** is about 0.035 oz.
A **milligram (mg)** is 1/1000 g or about 0.000035 oz.
A **kilogram (kg)** is 1,000 g or about 2.2 lb.
A **metric ton (t)** is 1,000 kg or about 1.1 tn.

To change g to mg, multiply by 1,000.
To change g to kg, divide by 1,000.
To change kg to g, multiply by 1,000.
To change t to kg, multiply by 1,000.

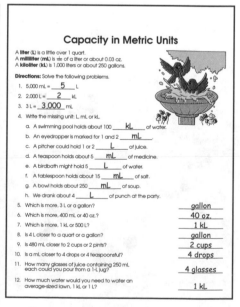

Directions: Solve the following problems.

1. 3 kg = _3,000_ g
2. 2 g = _2,000_ mg
3. 145 g = _0.145_ kg
4. 3,000 kg = _3_ t
5. _0.450_ g = 450 mg
6. 3.5 t = _3,500_ kg

7. Write the missing units below: g, mg, kg or t.

a. A sunflower seed weighs less than 1 _g_.
b. A serving of cereal contains 14 _g_ of sugar.
c. The same serving of cereal has 250 _mg_ of salt.
d. A bowling ball weighs about 7 _kg_.
e. A whale weighs about 90 _t_.
f. A math textbook weighs about 1 _kg_.
g. A safety pin weighs about 1 _g_.
h. An average car weighs about 1 _t_.

8. Is 200 g closer to 7 oz. or 70 oz.? _7 oz._
9. Is 3 kg closer to 7 lb. or 70 lb.? _7 lbs._
10. Does a metric ton weigh more or less than a ton measured by the customary system? _more_
11. How is a kilogram different from a kilometer? _A kilogram measures weight; a kilometer measures length._
12. Which is heavier, 300 g or 1 kg? _1 kg_

72

Capacity in Customary Units

Here are the main ways to measure capacity (how much something will hold) in customary units:

8 fluid ounces (fl. oz.) = 1 cup (c.)
2 c. = 1 pint (pt.)
2 pt. = 1 quart (qt.)
4 qt. = 1 gallon (gal.)

To change ounces to cups, divide by 8.
To change cups to ounces, multiply by 8.
To change cups to pints or quarts, divide by 2.
To change pints to cups or quarts to pints, multiply by 2.

As with measurements of length and weight, you may have to borrow units in subtraction.

Example:
```
  3 gal. 2 qt. = 2 gal. 6 qt.
- 1 gal. 3 qt. - 1 gal. 3 qt.
              1 gal. 3 qt.
```

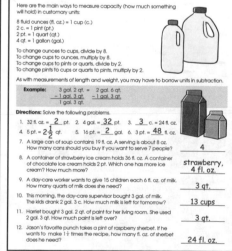

Directions: Solve the following problems.

1. 32 fl. oz. = _2_ c.
2. 4 gal. = _32_ pt.
3. _3_ c. = 24 fl. oz.
4. 5 pt. = _2 1/2_ qt.
5. 16 pt. = _2_ gal.
6. 3 pt. = _48_ fl. oz.

7. A large can of soup contains 19 fl. oz. A serving is about 8 oz. How many cans should you buy if you want to serve 7 people? _4_
8. A container of strawberry ice cream holds 36 fl. oz. A container of chocolate ice cream holds 2 pt. Which one has more ice cream? How much more? _strawberry, 4 fl. oz._
9. A day-care worker wants to give 15 children each 6 fl. oz. of milk. How many quarts of milk does she need? _3 qt._
10. This morning, the day-care supervisor bought 3 gal. of milk. The kids drank 2 gal. 3 c. How much milk is left for tomorrow? _13 cups_
11. Harriet bought 3 gal. 2 qt. of paint for her living room. She used 2 gal. 3 qt. How much paint is left over? _3 qt._
12. Jason's favorite punch takes a pint of raspberry sherbet. If he wants to make 1 1/2 times the recipe, how many fl. oz. of sherbet does he need? _24 fl. oz._

73

Capacity in Metric Units

A **liter (L)** is a little over 1 quart.
A **milliliter (mL)** is 1/1000 of a liter or about 0.03 oz.
A **kiloliter (kL)** is 1,000 liters or about 250 gallons.

Directions: Solve the following problems.

1. 5,000 mL = _5_ L
2. 2,000 L = _2_ kL
3. 3 L = _3,000_ mL

4. Write the missing unit: L, mL or kL.

a. A swimming pool holds about 100 _kL_ of water.
b. An eyedropper is marked for 1 or 2 _mL_.
c. A pitcher could hold 1 or 2 _L_ of juice.
d. A teaspoon holds about 5 _mL_ of medicine.
e. A birdbath might hold 5 _L_ of water.
f. A tablespoon holds about 15 _mL_ of salt.
g. A bowl holds about 250 _mL_ of soup.
h. We drank about 4 _L_ of punch at the party.

5. Which is more, 3 L or a gallon? _gallon_
6. Which is more, 400 mL or 40 oz.? _40 oz._
7. Which is more, 1 kL or 500 L? _1 kL_
8. Is 4 L closer to a quart or a gallon? _gallon_
9. Is 480 mL closer to 2 cups or 2 pints? _2 cups_
10. Is a mL closer to 4 drops or 4 teaspoonsful? _4 drops_
11. How many glasses of juice containing 250 mL each could you pour from a 1-L jug? _4 glasses_
12. How much water would you need to water an average-sized lawn, 1 kL or 1 L? _1 kL_

74

Temperature in Customary and Metric Units

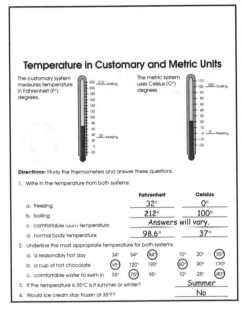

The customary system measures temperature in Fahrenheit (F°) degrees.

The metric system uses Celsius (C°) degrees.

Directions: Study the thermometers and answer these questions.

1. Write in the temperature from both systems:

	Fahrenheit	Celsius
a. freezing	32°	0°
b. boiling	212°	100°
c. comfortable room temperature	Answers will vary.	
d. normal body temperature	98.6°	37°

2. Underline the most appropriate temperature for both systems:

a. a reasonably hot day   34°   54°   (84°)   10°   20°   (35°)

b. a cup of hot chocolate   (95°)   120°   190°   (60°)   90°   120°

c. comfortable water to swim in   55°   (75°)   95°   10°   25°   (40°)

3. If the temperature is 35°C is it summer or winter?   Summer

4. Would ice cream stay frozen at 35°F?   No

75

Customary and Metric Measures

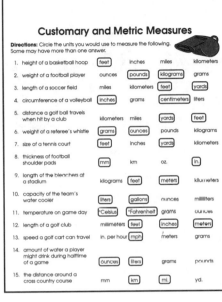

Directions: Circle the units you would use to measure the following. Some may have more than one answer.

1. height of a basketball hoop — (feet)   inches   miles   kilometers

2. weight of a football player — ounces   (pounds)   (kilograms)   grams

3. length of a soccer field — miles   kilometers   (feet)   (yards)

4. circumference of a volleyball — (inches)   grams   (centimeters)   liters

5. distance a golf ball travels when hit by a club — kilometers   miles   (yards)   (feet)

6. weight of a referee's whistle — (grams)   (ounces)   pounds   kilograms

7. size of a tennis court — (feet)   inches   (yards)   kilometers

8. thickness of a football shoulder pads — (mm)   km   oz.   (in.)

9. length of the bleachers at a stadium — kilograms   (feet)   (meters)   kilometers

10. capacity of the team's water cooler — (liters)   (gallons)   ounces   milliliters

11. temperature on game day — (°Celsius)   (°Fahrenheit)   grams   ounces

12. length of a golf club — millimeters   (feet)   (inches)   (meters)

13. speed a golf cart can travel — in. per hour   (mph)   meters   grams

14. amount of water a player might drink during halftime of a game — (ounces)   (liters)   grams   pounds

15. the distance around a cross country course — mm   (km)   (mi.)   yd.

76

Comparing Measurements

Directions: Use the symbols >, < or = to make the following statements true.

1. 1 oz. (>) 1 g   2. 10 kL (>) 100 L   3. 25 cm (<) 15 in.

4. 20 L (>) 40 oz.   5. 60 oz. (>) 2 lb.   6. 20 m (<) 2 mi.

7. 2 gal. (>) 2 L   8. 15 g (<) 25 oz.   9. 35 ft. (<) 12 yd.

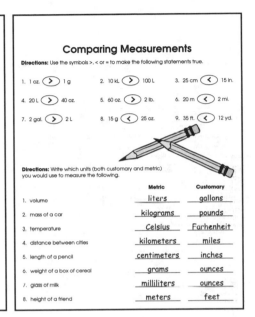

Directions: Write which units (both customary and metric) you would use to measure the following.

	Metric	Customary
1. volume	liters	gallons
2. mass of a car	kilograms	pounds
3. temperature	Celsius	Farhenheit
4. distance between cities	kilometers	miles
5. length of a pencil	centimeters	inches
6. weight of a box of cereal	grams	ounces
7. glass of milk	milliliters	ounces
8. height of a friend	meters	feet

77

Review

Directions: Complete the following exercises.

1. 372 in. = 10.33 yd.   31 ft.

2. 4 km = 4,000 m

3. 1.25 lb. = 20 oz.

4. 2,000 mg = 2 g

5. 1 qt. = 32 oz.

6. 10,000 mL = 10 L

7. Todd has a board that is 6 ft. 3 in. long. He needs to cut it to 4 ft. 9 in. How much should he cut off? — 18 in. (1 ft. 6 in.)

8. In a contest, Joyce threw a ball 12 yd. 2 ft. Brenda threw the ball 500 in. Who threw the farthest? — Brenda

9. Would you measure this workbook in mm or cm? — cm

10. Which is heavier, a box of books that weigh 4 lb. 6 oz. or a box of dishes that weigh 80 oz.? — 80 oz.

11. A 1-lb. package has 10 hot dogs. How much of an ounce does each hot dog weigh? — 1.6 oz.

12. Would the amount of salt (sodium) in 1 oz. of potato chips be 170 g or 170 mg? — 170 mg.

13. If someone ate half of a gallon of ice cream, how many fluid ounces would be left? — 64 fl. oz.

14. You want to serve 6 fl. oz. of ice cream to each of 16 friends at your party. How many quarts of ice cream should you buy? — 3 qt.

15. Would you measure water in a fish pond with L or kL? — kL

16. Would popsicles melt at 5°C? — Yes

17. Would soup be steaming hot at 100°F? — Yes

78

Ratios

A **ratio** is a comparison of two quantities. For example, a wall is 96 in. high; a pencil is 8 in. long. By dividing 8 into 96, you find it would take 12 pencils to equal the height of the wall. The ratio, or comparison, of the wall to the pencil can be written three ways:
1 to 12; 1:12; $\frac{1}{12}$. In this example, the ratio of triangles to circles is 4:6.
The ratio of triangles to squares is 4:9. The ratio of circles to squares is 6:9. These ratios will stay the same if we divide both numbers in the ratio by the same number.

Examples: $\frac{4 \div 2}{6 \div 2} = \frac{2}{3}$ $\frac{6 \div 3}{9 \div 3} = \frac{2}{3}$ (There is no number that will divide into both 4 and 9.)

By reducing 4:6 and 6:9 to their lowest terms, they are the same—2:3. This means that 2:3, 4:6 and 6:9 are all equal ratios. You can also find equal ratios for all three by multiplying both numbers of the ratio by the same number.

Examples: $\frac{4 \times 3}{6 \times 3} = \frac{12}{18}$ $\frac{6 \times 5}{9 \times 5} = \frac{30}{45}$ $\frac{4 \times 4}{9 \times 4} = \frac{16}{36}$

Directions: Solve the following problems.

1. Write two more equal ratios for each of the following by multiplying or dividing both numbers in the ratio by the same number.

a. $\frac{1}{2} \; \frac{2}{4} \; \frac{3}{6}$ $\frac{4}{8} \; \frac{5}{10}$ b. $\frac{2}{4} \; \frac{1}{8} \; \frac{3}{12}$ $\frac{5}{20}$ c. $\frac{8}{24} \; \frac{1}{3} \; \frac{2}{6}$ $\frac{4}{12}$

2. Circle the ratios that are equal.

a. $\frac{1}{6} \; \frac{3}{6}$ b. [$\frac{15}{25} \; \frac{3}{5}$]   c. [$\frac{6}{7} \; \frac{30}{35}$]   d. $\frac{2}{3} \; \frac{6}{10}$

3. Write each ratio three ways.

a. stars to crosses — 3:7, $^{3}/_{7}$, 3 to 7

b. crosses to trees — 7:5, $^{7}/_{5}$, 7 to 5

c. stars to all other shapes — 3 to 12, 3:12, $^{3}/_{12}$

4. Write two equal ratios (multiplying or dividing) for:

a. stars to crosses — $^{3}/_{7}$, $^{6}/_{14}$

b. crosses to trees — $^{7}/_{5}$, $^{14}/_{10}$

c. stars to all other shapes — $^{3}/_{12}$, $^{6}/_{24}$

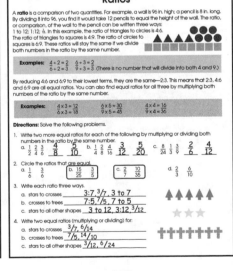

79

Missing Numbers in Ratios

You can find a missing number (n) in an equal ratio. First, figure out which number has already been multiplied to get the number you know. (In the first example, 3 is multiplied by 3 to get 9; in the second example, 2 is multiplied by 6 to get 12.) Then multiply the other number in the ratio by the same number (3 and 6 in the examples).

Examples: $\frac{3}{4} = \frac{9}{n}$ $\frac{3}{4} \times \frac{3}{3} = \frac{9}{12}$ $n = 12$ $\frac{1}{2} = \frac{n}{12}$ $\frac{1}{2} \times \frac{6}{6} = \frac{6}{12}$ $n = 6$

Directions: Solve the following problems.

1. Find each missing number.

a. $\frac{1}{2} = \frac{n}{12}$ $n = $ 6   b. $\frac{1}{5} = \frac{n}{15}$ $n = $ 3   c. $\frac{3}{2} = \frac{18}{n}$ $n = $ 12

d. $\frac{5}{8} = \frac{n}{32}$ $n = $ 20   e. $\frac{8}{3} = \frac{16}{n}$ $n = $ 6   f. $\frac{n}{14} = \frac{5}{7}$ $n = $ 10

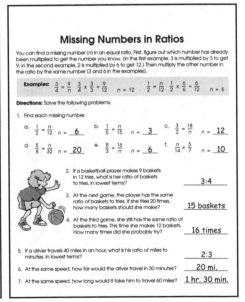

2. If a basketball player makes 9 baskets in 12 tries, what is her ratio of baskets to tries, in lowest terms? — 3:4

3. At the next game, the player has the same ratio of baskets to tries. If she tries 20 times, how many baskets should she make? — 15 baskets

4. At the third game, she still has the same ratio of baskets to tries. This time she makes 12 baskets. How many times did she probably try? — 16 times

5. If a driver travels 40 miles in an hour, what is his ratio of miles to minutes, in lowest terms? — 2:3

6. At the same speed, how far would the driver travel in 30 minutes? — 20 mi.

7. At the same speed, how long would it take him to travel 60 miles? — 1 hr. 30 min.

80

Ratio Review

Directions: Use the bird-watching data from the chart to complete the following exercises.

Species	Day 1	Day 2	Day 3
Robin	12	20	10
Cardinal	9	12	9
Sparrow	22	24	26
Blue Jay	7	7	14
Woodpecker	3	6	9
Purple Finch	5	10	5
House Wren	18	9	12

1. Find the ratio between the following sets of birds for all days.

   blue jay to cardinal   28   to   30

   robin to sparrow   42   to   72

   purple finch to house wren   20   to   39

   woodpecker to blue jay   18   to   38

2. State the ratio of each for the first and second day, and the second and third day.

   cardinal   9 to 12   and   12 to 9

   robin   12 to 20   and   20 to 10

   sparrow   22 to 24   and   24 to 26

   blue jay   7 to 7   and   7 to 14

   woodpecker   3 to 6   and   6 to 9

   purple finch   5 to 10   and   10 to 5

   house wren   18 to 9   and   9 to 12

3. Which birds have equivalent ratios?   woodpecker & purple finch

4. What process did you use to find the equal ratios?   division

5. How could you tell if two ratios are not equivalent?   They would not
reduce to the same fraction.

81

Proportions

A **proportion** is a statement that two ratios are equal, called a proportion, we multiply the cross products.

Examples of proportions: $\frac{1}{5} = \frac{2}{10}$ $\frac{1}{2} \times \frac{10}{5} = \frac{10}{10}$ $\frac{3}{7} = \frac{15}{35}$ $\frac{3}{7} \times \frac{35}{15} = \frac{105}{105}$

These two ratios are not a proportion: $\frac{4}{3} = \frac{5}{6}$ $\frac{4}{3} \times \frac{5}{6} = \frac{24}{15}$

To find a missing number (n) in a proportion, multiply the cross products and divide.

Examples: $\frac{n}{30} = \frac{1}{6}$ $n \times 6 = 1 \times 30$ $n \times 6 = 30$ $n = \frac{30}{6}$ $n = 5$

Directions: Solve the following problems.

1. Write = between the ratios if they are a proportion. Write ≠ if they are not a proportion. The first one has been done for you.

   a. $\frac{1}{2}$ = $\frac{6}{12}$ b. $\frac{13}{18}$ ≠ $\frac{20}{22}$ c. $\frac{2}{6}$ = $\frac{5}{15}$ d. $\frac{5}{6}$ = $\frac{20}{24}$

2. Find the missing numbers in these proportions.

   a. $\frac{2}{5} = \frac{n}{15}$ n = 6   b. $\frac{3}{8} = \frac{9}{n}$ n = 24   c. $\frac{n}{18} = \frac{4}{12}$ n = 6

3. One issue of a magazine costs $2.99, but if you buy a subscription, 12 issues cost $35.99. Is the price at the same proportion?   Yes

4. A cookie recipe calls for 3 cups of flour to make 36 cookies. How much flour is needed for 48 cookies?   4

5. The same recipe requires 4 teaspoons of cinnamon for 36 cookies. How many teaspoons is needed to make 48 cookies? (Answer will include a fraction.) $5\frac{1}{3}$

6. The recipe also calls for 2 cups of sugar for 36 cookies. How much sugar should you use for 48 cookies? (Answer will include a fraction.) $2\frac{33}{50}$

7. If 2 kids can eat 12 cookies, how many can 8 kids eat?   48

82

Percents

Percent means "per 100." A percent is a ratio that compares a number with 100. The same number can be written as a decimal and a percent. To change a decimal to a percent, move the decimal point two places to the right and add the % sign. To change a percent to a decimal, drop the % sign and place a decimal point two places to the left.

Examples: 0.25 = 25%   0.1 = 10%   1.456 = 145.6%
   32% = 0.32   99% = 0.99   203% = 2.03

A percent or decimal can also be written as a ratio or fraction.

Example: $0.25 = 25\% = \frac{25}{100} = \frac{1}{4} = 1:4$

To change a fraction or ratio to a percent, first change it to a decimal. Divide the numerator by the denominator.

Examples: $\frac{1}{3} = 3\overline{)1.00}^{0.33\frac{1}{3} = 33\frac{1}{3}\%}$ $\frac{2}{5} = 5\overline{)2.0}^{0.4 = 40\%}$

Directions: Solve the following problems.

1. Change the percents to decimals.

   a. 3% = 0.03   b. 75% = 0.75   c. 14% = 0.14   d. 115% = 1.15

2. Change the decimals and fractions to percents.

   a. 0.56 = 56 %   b. 0.03 = 3 %   c. $\frac{3}{4}$ = 75 %   d. $\frac{1}{5}$ = 20 %

3. Change the percents to ratios in their lowest terms. The first one has been done for you.

   a. 75% = $^{75}/_{100}$ = $^{3}/_4$ = 3:4   b. 40% = $^{40}/_{100}$ = $^2/_5$ = 2:5

   c. 35% = $^{35}/_{100} = ^7/_{20}$ = 7:20   d. 70% = $^{70}/_{100} = ^7/_{10}$ = 7:10

4. The class was 45% girls. What percent was boys?   55%

5. Half the shoes in one store were on sale. What percent of the shoes were their ordinary price?   50%

6. Kim read 84 pages of a 100-page book. What percent of the book did she read?   84%

83

Percents

To find the percent of a number, change the percent to a decimal and multiply.

Examples: 45% of $20 = 0.45 × $20 = $9.00
   125% of 30 = 1.25 × 30 = 37.50

Directions: Solve the following problems. Round off the answers to the nearest hundredth where necessary.

1. Find the percent of each number.

   a. 26% of 40 = 10.4   b. 12% of 329 = 39.48

   c. 73% of 19 = 13.87   d. 2% of 24 = 0.48

2. One family spends 35% of its weekly budget of $150 on food. How much do they spend? $52.50

3. A shirt in a store usually costs $15.99, but today it's on sale for 25% off. The clerk says you will save $4.50. Is that true?   No

4. A book that usually costs $12 is on sale for 25% off. How much will it cost? $9.00

5. After you answer 60% of 150 math problems, how many do you have left to do?   60

6. A pet store's shipment of tropical fish was delayed. Nearly 40% of the 1,350 fish died. About how many lived?   810

7. The shipment had 230 angelfish, which died in the same proportion as the other kinds of fish. About how many angelfish died?   92

8. A church youth group was collecting cans of food. Their goal was 1,200 cans, but they exceeded their goal by 25%. How many cans did they collect?   1,500

84

Percents

When working with percents, think of them as fractions with a denominator of 100. To calculate the percent of any number, first change the percent to a decimal and then multiply the two numbers.

Example: $15\% = \frac{15}{100}$ 15% of 25 = 0.15 × 25 = 3.75

Directions: Solve the following problems.

1. Brian collected 93 buckeyes from a tree in his grandmother's yard. He wanted to share some of them with his friends at school. If he gave away 40, what percent did he keep for himself?   57%

2. As part of a science project, Brian planted 10 buckeyes on Saturday and 6 more on the following Tuesday. Two weeks later, 4 tiny sprouts emerged from the soil. When Brian wrote his science report, he listed his project as having a success rate of what percent?   25%

3. While sorting the buckeyes, Brian found that only 7% of them had a diameter larger than 1.5 inches, 31% had a diameter of about 1 inch and the remaining 62% were less than 1 inch. How many buckeyes were in each group?   7%=6, 31%=29, 62%=58

4. Brian used 30 buckeyes to make keychains for a craft show. It took him $\frac{1}{3}$ of an hour to make each one. He finished 9 of them the first day. What percent of the project did he have done and how much time will he need to complete the whole project?   30 %   time: 7 hrs., 30 min.

5. Brian wanted to earn money to buy a science book about buckeye trees. He sold the keychains for $3 each at the craft show and collected $60. What percent of his product did he have left?   33%

6. Calculate the percentages.

   60% of 99 = 59.4   30% of 49 = 14.7   75% of 12 = 9

   29% of 100 = 29   20% of 250 = 50   17% of 175 = 29.75

85

Probability

Probability is the ratio of favorable outcomes to possible outcomes in an experiment. You can use probability (P) to figure out how likely something is to happen. For example, six picture cards are turned facedown—3 cards have stars, 2 have triangles and 1 has a circle. What is the probability of picking the circle? Using the formula below, you have a 1 in 6 probability of picking the circle, a 2 in 6 probability of picking a triangle and a 3 in 6 probability of picking a star.

Example: $P = \frac{\text{number of favorable outcomes}}{\text{number of trials}}$ $P = \frac{1}{6} = 1:6$

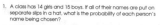

Directions: Solve the following problems.

1. A class has 14 girls and 15 boys. If all of their names are put on separate slips in a hat, what is the probability of each person's name being chosen?   1:29

2. In the same class, what is the probability that a girl's name will be chosen?   14:29

3. In this class, 3 boys are named Mike. What is the probability that a slip with "Mike" written on it will be chosen?   3:29

4. A spinner on a board game has the numbers 1–8. What is the probability of spinning and getting a 4?   1:8

5. A paper bag holds these colors of wooden beads: 4 blue, 5 red and 6 yellow. If you select a bead without looking, do you have an equal probability of getting each color?   No

6. Using the same bag of beads, what is the probability of reaching in and drawing out a red bead (in lowest terms)?   1:3

7. In the same bag, what is the probability of not getting a blue bead?   2:1

8. In a carnival game, plastic ducks have spots. The probability of picking a duck with a yellow spot is 2:15. There is twice as much probability of picking a duck with a red spot. What is the probability of picking a duck with a red spot?   4:15

9. In this game, all the other ducks have green spots. What is the probability of picking a duck with a green spot (in lowest terms)?   3:5

86

Possible Combinations

Today the cafeteria is offering 4 kinds of sandwiches, 3 kinds of drinks and 2 kinds of cookies. How many possible combinations could you make? To find out, multiply the number of choices together.

Example: $4 \times 3 \times 2 = 24$ possible combinations

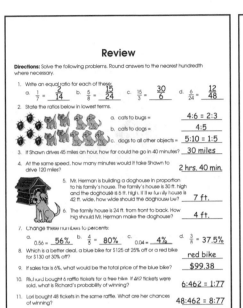

Directions: Solve the following problems.

1. If Juan has 3 shirts and 4 pairs of shorts, how many combinations can he make? **12**

2. Janice can borrow 1 book and 1 magazine at a time from her classroom library. The library has 45 books and 16 magazines. How many combinations are possible? **720**

3. Kerry's mother is redecorating the living room. She has narrowed her choices to 6 kinds of wallpaper, 3 shades of paint and 4 colors of carpeting that all match. How many possible combinations are there? **72**

4. Pam has 6 sweaters that she can combine with pants to make 24 outfits. How many pairs of pants does she have? **4**

5. Kenny can get to school by walking, taking a bus, riding his bike or asking his parents for a ride. He can get home the same ways, except his parents aren't available then. How many combinations can he make of ways to get to school and get home? **12**

6. Sue's middle school offers 3 different language classes, 3 art classes and 2 music classes. If she takes one class in each area, how many possible combinations are there? **18**

7. Bart's school offers 4 language classes, 3 art classes and some music classes. If Bart can make 36 possible combinations, how many music classes are there? **3**

8. AAA Airlines schedules 12 flights a day from Chicago to Atlanta. Four of those flights go on to Orlando. From the Orlando airport you can take a bus, ride in a taxi or rent a car to get to Disneyworld. How many different ways are there to get from Chicago to Disneyworld if you make part of your trip on AAA Airlines? **12**

87

Review

Directions: Solve the following problems. Round answers to the nearest hundredth where necessary.

1. Write an equal ratio for each of these:
   a. $\frac{1}{7} = \frac{2}{14}$
   b. $\frac{5}{8} = \frac{15}{24}$
   c. $\frac{15}{3} = \frac{30}{6}$
   d. $\frac{6}{24} = \frac{12}{48}$

2. State the ratios below in lowest terms.
   a. cats to bugs = **4:6 = 2:3**
   b. cats to dogs = **4:5**
   c. dogs to all other objects = **5:10 = 1:5**

3. If Shawn drives 45 miles an hour, how far could he go in 40 minutes? **30 miles**

4. At the same speed, how many minutes would it take Shawn to drive 120 miles? **2 hrs. 40 min.**

5. Mr. Herman is building a doghouse in proportion to his family's house. The family's house is 30 ft. high and the doghouse is 6 ft. high. If the family house is 42 ft. wide, how wide should the doghouse be? **7 ft.**

6. The family house is 24 ft. from front to back. How big should Mr. Herman make the doghouse? **4 ft.**

7. Change these numbers to percents:
   a. $0.56 =$ **56%**
   b. $\frac{4}{5} =$ **80%**
   c. $0.04 =$ **4%**
   d. $\frac{3}{8} =$ **37.5%**

8. Which is a better deal, a blue bike for $125 at 25% off or a red bike for $130 at 30% off? **red bike**

9. If sales tax is 6%, what would be the total price of the blue bike? **$99.38**

10. Richard bought 6 raffle tickets for a free hike. If 462 tickets were sold, what is Richard's probability of winning? **6:462 = 1:77**

11. Lori bought 48 tickets in the same raffle. What are her chances of winning? **48:462 = 8:77**

88

Review

Directions: Follow the instructions below. Write >, < or =.

1. $\frac{20}{25} \boxed{>} \frac{3}{5}$
2. $\frac{1}{7} \boxed{<} \frac{7}{28}$
3. $\frac{1}{3} \boxed{=} \frac{8}{24}$

Find the missing numbers.

1. $\frac{1}{3} = \frac{n}{15}$ n = **5**
2. $\frac{4}{5} = \frac{16}{n}$ n = **20**
3. $\frac{1}{14} = \frac{1}{7}$ n = **2**

Find the answers.

1. 30% of 25 = **7.5**
2. 64% of 100 = **64**
3. 16% of 47 = **7.5**
4. 75% of 60 = **45**

Change the percents to ratios.

1. 50% **1:2**
2. 80% **4:5**
3. 20% **1:5**
4. 35% **7:20**

While getting dressed for school early one morning, the light in Toni's bedroom burned out. Toni knew he had plenty of clean socks in his drawer, but none of them were matched. He had 24 white socks and 6 blue socks. What is the probability of Toni finding 2 white socks or 2 blue socks in the dark?

white **24:6 or 4:1**   blue **6:24 or 1:4**

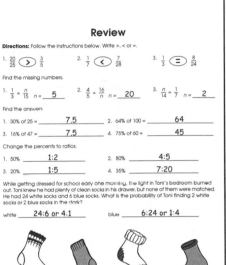

89

Comparing Data

Data (datum—singular) are gathered information. The **range** is the difference between the highest and lowest number in a group of numbers. The **median** is the number in the middle when numbers are listed in order. The **mean** is the average of the numbers. We can compare numbers or data by finding the range, median and mean.

Example: 16, 43, 34, 78, 8, 91, 26

To compare these numbers, we first need to put them in order: 8 16 26 34 43 78 91. By subtracting the lowest number (8) from the highest one (91), we find the range: 83. By finding the number that falls in the middle, we have the median: 34 (If no number fell exactly in the middle, we would average the two middle numbers.) By adding them and dividing by the number of numbers (7), we get the mean: 42.29 (rounded to the nearest hundredth).

Directions: Solve the following problems. Round answers to the nearest hundredth where necessary.

1. Find the range, median and mean of these numbers: 19, 5, 84, 27, 106, 38, 75.
   Range: **101**   Median: **38**   Mean: **50.57**

2. Find the range, median and mean finishing times for 6 runners in a race. Here are their times in seconds: 14.2, 12.9, 13.5, 10.3, 14.8, 14.7.
   Range: **4.5**   Median: **13.85**   Mean: **13.4**

3. If the runner who won the race in 10.3 seconds had run even faster and finished in 7 seconds, would the mean time be higher or lower? **Lower**

4. If that runner had finished in 7 seconds, what would be the median time? **13.85 (same)**

5. Here are the high temperatures in one city for a week: 65, 72, 68, 74, 81, 68, 85. Find the range, median and mean temperatures.
   Range: **20**   Median: **72**   Mean: **73.29**

6. Find the range, median and mean test scores for this group of students: 41, 32, 45, 36, 48, 38, 37, 42, 39, 36.
   Range: **16**   Median: **38.5**   Mean: **39.4**

90

Tables

Organizing data into tables makes it easier to compare numbers. As evident in the example, putting many numbers in a paragraph is confusing. When the same numbers are organized in a table, you can compare numbers in a glance. Tables can be arranged several ways and still be easy to read and understand.

Example: Money spent on groceries:
Family A: week 1 — $68.50; week 2 — $72.25; week 3 — $67.00; week 4 — $74.50.
Family B: week 1 — $42.25; week 2 — $47.50; week 3 — $50.25; week 4 — $53.50.

	Week 1	Week 2	Week 3	Week 4
Family A	$68.50	$72.25	$67.00	$74.50
Family B	$45.25	$47.50	$50.25	$53.50

Directions: Complete the following exercises.

1. Finish the table below, then answer the questions.
   Data: Steve weighs 230 lb. and is 6 ft. 2 in. tall. George weighs 218 lb. and is 6 ft. 3 in. tall. Chuck weighs 225 lb. and is 6 ft. 1 in. tall. Henry weighs 205 lb. and is 6 ft. tall.

	Henry	George	Chuck	Steve
Weight	205 lbs.	218 lbs.	225 lbs.	230 lbs.
Height	6 ft.	6 ft. 3 in.	6 ft. 1 in.	6 ft. 2 in.

   a. Who is tallest? **George**   b. Who weighs the least? **Henry**

2. On another sheet of paper, prepare 2 tables comparing the amount of money made by 3 booths at the school carnival this year and last year. In the first table, write the names of the games in the left-hand column (like **Family A** and **Family B** in the example). In the second table (using the same data), write the years in the left-hand column. Here is the data: fish pond—this year $15.60, last year $13.50; bean-bag toss—this year $13.45, last year $10.25; ring toss—this year $23.80, last year $18.80. After you complete both tables, answer the following questions.
   a. Which booth made the most money this year? **ring toss**
   b. Which booth made the biggest improvement from last year to this year? **ring toss**

91

Bar Graphs

Another way to organize information is a **bar graph**. The bar graph in the example compares the number of students in 4 elementary schools. Each bar stands for 1 school. You can easily see that School A has the most students and School C has the least. The numbers along the left show how many students attend each school.

Example:

Directions: Complete the following exercises.

1. This bar graph will show how many calories are in 1 serving of 4 kinds of cereal. Draw the bars the correct height and label each with the name of the cereal. After completing the bar graph, answer the questions. Data: Korn Kernals—150 calories; Oat Floats—160 calories; Rite Rice—110 calories; Sugar Shapes—200 calories.

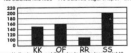

   A. Which cereal is the best to eat if you're trying to lose weight? **Rite Rice**
   B. Which cereal has nearly the same number of calories as Oat Floats? **Korn Kernals**

2. On another sheet of paper, draw your own graph, showing the number of TV commercials in 1 week for each of the 4 cereals in the graph above. After completing the graph, answer the questions. Data: Oat Boats—27 commercials; Rite Rice—15; Sugar Shapes—35; Korn Kernals—28.
   A. Which cereal is most heavily advertised? **Sugar Shapes**
   B. What similarities do you notice between the graph of calories and the graph of **Sugar Shapes is highest in sugar and advertisements**

92

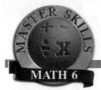

Picture Graphs

Newspapers and textbooks often use pictures in graphs instead of bars. Each picture stands for a certain number of objects. Half a picture means half the number. The picture graph in the example indicates the number of games each team won. The Astros won 7 games, so they have $3\frac{1}{2}$ balls.

Example:

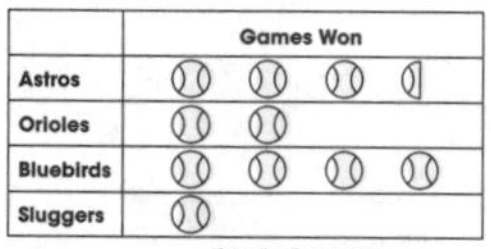

Games Won
Astros
Orioles
Bluebirds
Sluggers

(1 ball = 2 games)

Directions: Complete the following exercises.

Finish this picture graph, showing the number of students who have dogs in 4 sixth-grade classes. Draw simple dogs in the graph, letting each drawing stand for 2 dogs. Data: Class 1—12 dogs; Class 2—16 dogs; Class 3—22 dogs; Class 4—12 dogs. After completing the graph, answer the questions.

	Dogs Owned by Students
Class 1	○○○○○○
Class 2	○○○○○○○○
Class 3	○○○○○○○○○○○
Class 4	○○○○○○

(One dog drawing = 2 students' dogs)

1. Why do you think newspapers use picture graphs? Answers will vary. It simplifies information and is easier to read.
2. Would picture graphs be appropriate to show exact number of dogs living in America? Why or why not? There are too many!

93

Line Graphs

Still another way to display information is a line graph. The same data can often be shown in both a bar graph and a line graph. Nevertheless, line graphs are especially useful in showing changes over a period of time.

The line graph in the example shows changes in the number of students enrolled in a school over a 5-year period. Enrollment was highest in 1988 and has decreased gradually each year since then. Notice how labeling the years and enrollment numbers make the graph easy to understand.

Example:

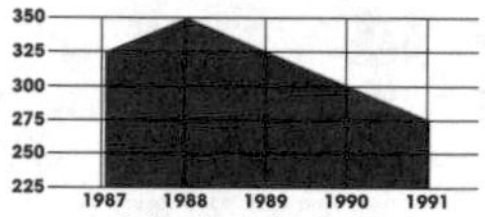

350
325
300
275
250
225
1987
1988
1989
1990
1991

Fall Enrollment at Cedar School

Directions: Complete the following exercises.

1. On another sheet of paper, draw a line graph that displays the growth of a corn plant over a 6-week period. Mark the correct points, using the data below, and connect them with a line. After completing the graph, answer the questions. Data: week 1—3.5 in.; week 2—4.5 in.; week 3—5 in.; week 4—5.5 in.; week 5—5.75 in.; week 6—6 in.
   a. Between which weeks was the growth fastest? 1 and 2
   b. Between which weeks was the growth slowest? 4 and 5; 5 and 6
2. On another sheet of paper draw a line graph to show how the high temperature varied during one week. Then answer the questions. Data: Sunday—high of 53 degrees; Monday—51; Tuesday—56; Wednesday—60; Thursday—58; Friday—67; Saturday—73. Don't forget to label the numbers.
   a. In general, did the days get warmer or cooler? warmer
   b. Do you think this data would have been as clear in a bar graph? No
   Explain your answer. Line graphs show a trend up and down across the graph.

94

Circle Graphs

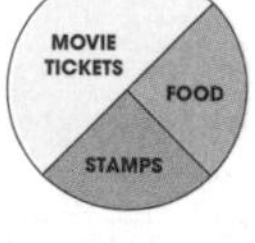

MOVIE TICKETS
FOOD
STAMPS

Circle graphs are useful in showing how something is divided into parts. The circle graph in the example shows how Carly spent her $10 allowance. Each section is a fraction of her whole allowance. For example, the movie tickets section is $\frac{1}{2}$ of the circle, showing that she spent $\frac{1}{2}$ of her allowance, $5, on movie tickets.

Directions: Complete the following exercises.

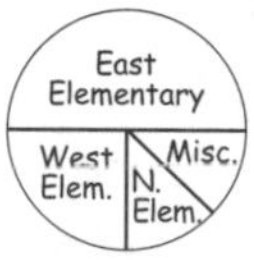

East Elementary
West Elem.
N. Elem.
Misc.

1. When the middle school opened last fall, $\frac{1}{2}$ of the students came from East Elementary, $\frac{1}{4}$ came from West Elementary, $\frac{1}{8}$ came from North Elementary and the remaining students moved into the town from other cities. Make a circle graph showing these proportions. Label each section. Then answer the questions.
   a. What fraction of students at the new school moved into the area from other cities? $\frac{1}{8}$
   b. If the new middle school has 450 students enrolled, how many used to go to East Elementary? 225

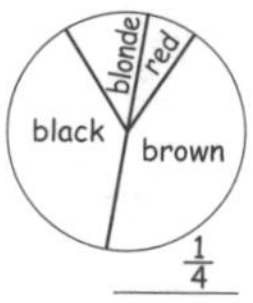

black
blonde
red
brown

2. This circle graph will show the hair color of 24 students in one class. Divide the circle into 4 sections to show this data: black hair—8 students; brown hair—10 students; blonde hair—4 students; red hair—2 students. (Hint: 8 students are $\frac{8}{24}$ or $\frac{1}{3}$ of the class.) Be sure to label each section by hair color. Then answer the questions.
   a. Looking at your graph, what fraction of the class is the combined group of blonde- and red-haired students? $\frac{1}{4}$
   b. Which two fractions of hair color combine to total half the class? red/brown

95

Comparing Presentation Methods

Tables and different kinds of graphs have different purposes. Some are more helpful for certain kinds of information. The table and three graphs below all show basically the same information—the amount of money Mike and Margaret made in their lawn-mowing business over a 4-month period.

Combined Income per Month

	Mike	Margaret
June	$34	$36
July	41	35
August	27	28
Sept.	36	40
Totals	$138	$139

Combined Income per Month

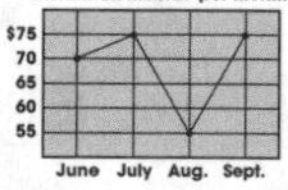

$75
70
65
60
55
June
July
Aug.
Sept.

Combined Income per Month

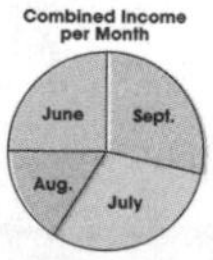

June
Sept.
Aug.
July

Combined Income per Month

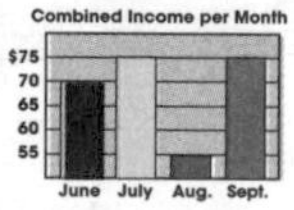

$75
70
65
60
55
June
July
Aug.
Sept.

Directions: Study the graphs and table. Then circle the one that answers each question below.

1. Which one shows the fraction of the total income that Mike and Margaret made in August?
   table line graph bar graph (circle graph)
2. Which one compares Mike's earnings with Margaret's?
   (table) line graph bar graph circle graph
3. Which one has the most exact numbers?
   (table) line graph bar graph circle graph
4. Which one has no numbers?
   table line graph bar graph (circle graph)
5. Which two best show how Mike and Margaret's income changed from month to month?
   table (line graph) (bar graph) circle graph

96

Graphing Data

Directions: Complete the following exercises.

1. Use the following information to create a bar graph.

Cities	Population (in 1,000's)
Dover	20
Newton Falls	12
Springdale	25
Hampton	17
Riverside	5

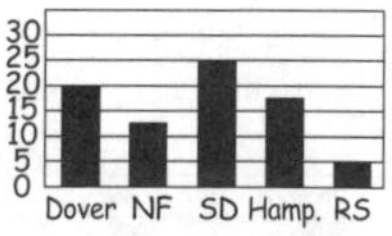

30
25
20
15
10
5
0
Dover
NF
SD
Hamp.
RS

2. Study the data and create a line graph showing the number of baskets Jonah scored during the season.

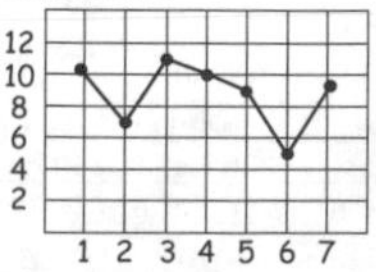

12
10
8
6
4
2
1 2 3 4 5 6 7

Game 1 — 10
Game 2 — 7
Game 3 — 11
Game 4 — 10
Game 5 — 9
Game 6 — 5
Game 7 — 9

Fill in the blanks.
a. High game: 3
b. Low game: 6
c. Average baskets per game: 8.7

3. Study the graph, then answer the questions.
   a. Which flavor is the most popular? chocolate
   b. Which flavor sold the least? Blue Moon
   c. What decimal represents the two highest sellers? 0.75
   d. Which flavor had $\frac{1}{10}$ of the sales? vanilla

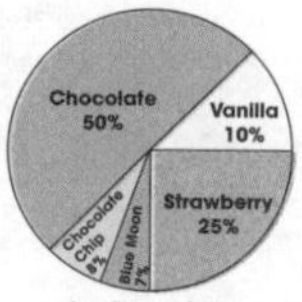

Chocolate 50%
Vanilla 10%
Strawberry 25%
Blue Moon 7%
Chocolate Chip 8%

Ice-Cream Sales

97

Review

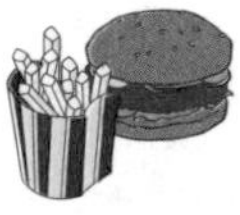

Directions: Complete the following exercises.

1. Joseph's older sister and 3 of her friends work at fast-food restaurants. Here is what they each make an hour: $3.85, $4.20, $3.95, $4.65. Find the range, median and mean of their earnings.
   range: $0.80 median: $4.08 mean: $4.16
2. If the person who makes $3.85 gets a 5-cent raise, what will be the median? $4.08 (same)
3. Write **T** for true or **F** for false:
   a. If you include dates in a table, you must write them across the top or bottom of the table, not in the left-hand column. T
   b. Tables allow you to show small differences between numbers. F
   c. A bar graph allows you to compare the amount of alcohol in different kinds of liquor. T
   d. A bar graph allows you to show small differences between numbers. T
   e. Picture graphs are used only in children's books. F
   f. Each picture in a picture graph equals one unit of something, such as one gallon of oil or one person. F
   g. Some kinds of information can be shown equally well in both a bar graph and a line graph. T
   h. Labeling types of information on a graph is not necessary because the reader can figure it out. F
   i. A line graph allows you to show changes in the popularity of a TV show month by month. T
   j. A circle graph is a good way to show changes in the popularity of a TV show over time. F

98

Integers

An **integer** is a whole number above or below 0: -2, -1, 0, +1, +2, and so on. **Opposite integers** are two integers the same distance from 0, but in different directions, such as -2 and +2.

Think of the water level in the picture as 0. The part of the iceberg sticking out of the water is positive. The iceberg has +3 feet above water. The part of the iceberg below the water is negative. The iceberg extends -9 feet under water.

Numbers greater than 0 are **positive** numbers. Numbers less than 0 are **negative** numbers. Pairs of positive and negative numbers are called **opposite integers**.

Examples of opposite integers:
-5 and +5
losing 3 pounds and gaining 3 pounds
earning $12 and spending $12

Directions: Complete the following exercises.

1. Write each of these as an integer. The first one is done for you.
   a. positive 6 = +6   b. losing $5 = -$5
   c. 5 degrees below 0 = -5   d. receiving $12 = +$12

2. Write the **opposite** integer of each of these. The first one is done for you.
   a. negative 4 = +4   b. positive 10 = -10
   c. 2 floors below ground level = +2   d. winning a card game by 6 points = -6

3. Write integers to show each idea.
   a. A train that arrives 2 hours after it was scheduled: -2
   b. A package that has 3 fewer cups than it should: -3
   c. A board that's 3 inches too short: -3   d. A golf score 5 over par: +5
   e. A paycheck that doesn't cover $35 of a family's expenses: -$35
   f. 30 seconds before a missile launch: -30
   g. A team that won 6 games and lost 2: +4

99

Comparing Integers

Comparing two integers can be confusing unless you think of them as being on a number line, as shown below. Remember that the integer farther to the right is greater. Thus, +2 is greater than -3, 0 is greater than -4 and -2 is greater than -5.

-5 -4 -3 -2 -1 0 +1 +2 +3 +4 +5

Directions: Study the number line. Then complete the following exercises.

1. Write in integers to complete the number line.

   -5 -4 -3 -2 -1 0 +1 +2 +3 +4 +5

2. Write < for "less than" or > for "greater than" to compare the integers. The first one is done for you.
   a. -5 < +5   b. +3 > -3   c. +2 > -4
   d. -4 < -3   e. -1 < +3   f. -1 > -5

3. Write **T** for true or **F** for false. (All degrees are in Fahrenheit.)
   a. +7 degrees is colder than -3 degrees. ___ F
   b. -14 degrees is colder than -7 degrees. ___ T
   c. +23 degrees is colder than -44 degrees. ___ F
   d. -5 degrees is colder than +4 degrees. ___ T

4. Draw an **X** by the series of integers that are in order from least to greatest.
   ___ +2, +3, -4
   X -3, 0, +1
   X -7, -4, -1
   ___ -3, -4, -5

100

Adding Integers

The sum of two positive integers is a positive integer.
Thus, +4 + +1 = +5.
The sum of two negative integers is a negative integer.
Thus, -5 + -2 = -7.
The sum of a positive and a negative integer has the sign of the integer that is farther from 0.
Thus, -5 + +3 = -3.
The sum of opposite integers is 0.
Thus, +2 + -2 = 0

Directions: Complete the following exercises.

1. Add these integers.
   a. +2 + +7 = +9   b. -4 + -2 = -6   c. +5 + -3 = +2   d. +4 + -4 = 0
   e. -10 + -2 = -12   f. +6 + -1 = +5   g. +45 + -30 = +15   h. -39 + +26 = -13

2. Write the problems as integers. The first one has been done for you.
   a. One cold morning, the temperature was -14 degrees. The afternoon high was 20 degrees warmer. What was the high temperature that day?
   -14 + +20 = +6
   b. Another day, the high temperature was 26 degrees, but the temperature dropped 35 degrees during the night. What was the low that night?
   +26 + -35 = -9
   c. Sherri's allowance was $7. She paid $4 for a movie ticket. How much money did she have left?
   +$7 + -$4 = +$3
   d. The temperature in a meat freezer was -10 degrees, but the power went off and the temperature rose 6 degrees. How cold was the freezer then?
   -10 + +6 = -4
   e. The school carnival took in $235, but it had expenses of $185. How much money did the carnival make after paying its expenses?
   +$235 + -$185 = +$50

101

Subtracting Integers

To subtract an integer, change its sign to the opposite and add it. If you are subtracting a negative integer, make it positive and add it: +4 + -6 = +4 +6 = +10. If you are subtracting a positive integer, make it negative and add it: +8 - +2 = +8 + -2 = +6.

More examples: -5 - -8 = -5 + +8 = +3
+3 - +7 = +3 + -7 = -4

Directions: Complete the following exercises.

1. Before subtracting these integers, rewrite each problem. The first one has been done for you.
   -6 - -8 = -6 + +8 = +2   +3 - -4 = +3 + +4 = +7
   +9 + -3 = +9 + -3 = +6   -1 - -7 = -1 + +7 = +6
   +7 - -5 = +7 + +5 = +12   -4 - +3 = -4 + -3 = -7

2. Write these problems as integers. The first one is done for you.
   a. The high temperature in the Arctic Circle one day was -42 degrees. The low was -67 degrees. What was the difference between the two?
   -42 - -67 = -42 + +67 = +25
   b. At the equator one day, the high temperature was +106 degrees. The low was +85 degrees. What was the difference between the two?
   +106 - +85 = +106 + -85 = +21
   c. At George's house one morning, the thermometer showed it was +7 degrees. The radio announcer said it was -2 degrees. What is the difference between the two temperatures?
   +7 - -2 = +7 + +2 = +9
   d. What is the difference between a temperature of +11 degrees and a wind-chill factor of -15 degrees?
   +11 - -15 = +11 + +15 = +26
   e. During a dry spell, the level of a river dropped from 3 feet above normal to 13 feet below normal. How many feet did it drop?
   +3 - -13 = +3 + +13 = +16
   f. Here are the average temperatures in a meat freezer for four days: -12, -11, -14 and -9 degrees. What is the difference between the highest and lowest temperature?
   -14 - -9 = -14 + +9 = -5

102

More Integers

Directions: Use the number line to help you complete the following exercises.

-8 -7 -6 -5 -4 -3 -2 -1 0 +1 +2 +3 +4 +5 +6 +7 +8

1. Write the following as integers:
   positive 5 +5   gain of 14 +14   negative 3 -3
   loss of 9 -9   positive 20 +20   negative 17 -17

2. Solve the following problems.
   +4 + +12 = +16   +32 + -10 = +22
   -7 + +1 = -6   -21 + -5 = -26
   +10 + -10 = 0   +15 + -10 = +5

3. Write the integers in order from lowest to highest.

	lowest			highest
+4, -7, +3, 0	-7	0	+3	+4
-18, +5, -11, +1	-18	-11	+1	+5
-8, -10, -2, -14	-14	-10	-8	-2
+2, -3, +9, -10	-10	-3	+2	+9

4. Find the difference between the following:
   -22 and -17 = -5   +38 and -27 = +65
   -45 and +6 = -51   -25 and -11 = -14
   +4 and -4 = 0   -13 and -3 = -10

103

Plotting Graphs

A graph with horizontal and vertical number lines can show the location of certain points. The horizontal number line is called the **x axis**, and the vertical number line is called the **y axis**. Two numbers, called the **x coordinate** and the **y coordinate**, show where a point is on the graph.

The first coordinate, x, tells how many units to the right or left of 0 the point is located. On the example graph, point A is +2, two units to the right of 0.

The second coordinate, y, tells how many units above or below 0 the point is located. On the example, point A is -3, three units below 0.

Thus, the coordinates of A are +2, -3. The coordinates of B are -3, +2. (Notice the order of the coordinates.) The coordinates of C are +3, +1; and D, -2, -2.

Directions: Study the example. Then answer these questions about the graph below.

1. What towns are at these coordinates?
   +1, +3   Patterson
   +1, -3   Harlow
   -4, +1   Stewart
   -2, -3   Clinton
   -3, -2   Weston
   -3, +3   Hillsville

2. What are the coordinates of these towns?
   Hampton   -2, +1
   Wooster   +3, +2
   Beachwood +2, -4
   Middletown +1, +1
   Kirby   -4, -1
   Arbor   +3, -2

104

Ordered Pairs

Ordered pairs is another term used to describe pairs of integers used to locate points on a graph.

Directions: Complete the following exercises.

1. Place the following points on the graph, using the ordered pairs as data.

+3, +3
-2, +4
+1, -2
+4, -3
-4, -4
+2, +3
-1, +4

2. Create your own set of ordered pairs. Use your home as the center of your coordinates—zero. Let the x axis serve as East and West. The y axis will be North and South. Now select things to plot on your graph—the school, playground, grocery store, a friend's house, and so on.

Place	Ordered pair of coordi...
School	
Grocer...	
Playgrou...	
Friend's h...	

Answers will vary.

105

Review

Directions: Complete the following exercises.

1. Write the **opposite** integers of the following:
   a. 14 degrees above 0 __-14__
   b. Spending $21 __+$21__

2. Write integers to show these ideas.
   a. 4 seconds after the launch of the space shuttle __+4__
   b. A lake 3 feet below its usual level __-3__
   c. 2 days before your birthday __-2__

3. Write < for "less than" or > for "greater than" to compare these integers.
   -2 __>__ -4   +2 __>__ -3   -1 __<__ +1

4. Add the integers.
   -14 + -11 = __-25__   -6 + +5 = __-1__   -7 + +7 = __0__

5. Subtract the integers.
   -4 - -5 = __+1__   +3 - -6 = __+9__   +7 - +2 = __+5__

6. Write **T** for true or **F** for false.
   a. The x coordinate is on the horizontal number line. __T__
   b. Add the x and y coordinates to find the location of a point. __F__
   c. Always state the x coordinate first. __T__
   d. A y coordinate of +2 would be above the horizontal number line. __T__
   e. An x coordinate of +2 would be to the right of the vertical number line. __T__

CERTIFICATE

Congratulations to

_____
(Your Name)

for finishing this workbook!

_____
(Date)

106

Teaching Suggestions

Estimating

Take your child to the grocery store with you. While shopping, ask him/her to compare the prices of similar items of varying sizes and determine which is the better bargain. Invite your child to look at labels, pointing out that many are listed with customary and metric measurements. Ask him/her to estimate the total cost of the items by rounding numbers and averaging. Tell your child how much money you have to spend, and ask him/her to estimate the amount of change you should receive.

Take the family out to dinner and have your child estimate the bill and then calculate the appropriate amount to leave for a tip.

Take your child to a shopping mall in which several stores are having sales. Ask your child to estimate how much 40%, 25%, 15%, and so on, off of an item would be. Then calculate the sale price.

Graphing

With your child, collect data at home of birds, insects, flowers, plants, and so on, which you see in your backyard. Do this on several different occasions, then find the ratio between the sets of data.

Invite your child to make charts of toys, books or music owned by different family members. Any topic will work! Arrange the data into charts or line graphs.

Have your child record the ages of all the family members, including grandparents, aunts, uncles and cousins. Then have him/her calculate the mean age of the family. Point out to your child how this differs from the median age, using the same set of numbers.

Geometry

Ask your child to be on the lookout for geometric shapes. Challenge him/her to find them at home and in the neighborhood. For example: the kitchen table is a rectangle; the rug is an oval; the mirror is a circle; the garden is a square.

Have your child cut out geometric shapes from cereal boxes, wallpaper scraps, construction paper, and so on. Invite him/her to create unique designs, and discuss the differences and similarities among the shapes.

Invite the whole family to join in measuring activities. See how quickly each family member can find the perimeter and area of his/her bedroom. Then figure out the volumes.

Invite your child to figure out how many square feet of living space are in your home, and how much space is used as storage areas.

Ask your child to figure out the dimensions of your roof. Point out that all he/she needs to do is know the perimeter of the house and the amount of overhang of the roof, which he/she can estimate. Ask your child to use both customary and metric measurements.

Design a flower bed or plant a vegetable garden. Ask your child to figure the dimensions needed for each plant, what percentage of the garden will be used for flowers, the ratio of edible plants to flowering plants, whether you will plant in straight lines or in geometric patterns, and so on.

Fractions

Cut up fruits, vegetables and other foods to help your child with the concept of fractions. Example: 8 sections of one whole orange — $\frac{1}{8}$, $\frac{8}{8}$; 2 halves of an apple — $\frac{1}{2}$, $\frac{2}{2}$; 6 pieces of pizza — $\frac{1}{6}$, $\frac{6}{6}$.

Your child can also use toy blocks in sets of 10, with a total of 100. Place the blocks on the floor and explain that this represents one whole. Select different fractions for your child to find.

Decimals

Have your child use money to understand the concept of decimals as part of a whole. Use dollar bills and a variety of coins. Ask your child to find various fractions, or parts, of a dollar. You and your child can write out "money problems" for each other to figure out. Also use money as a cross-reference with fractions. Example: 25 cents is 0.25 of a dollar. 25 cents is also $\frac{25}{100}$ of a dollar.